C000050268

theguardian
BOOK OF PLAYLISTS

theguardian

BOOK ▶F
PLAYLISTS

The Best of the *Guardian*'s 'Readers Recommend'

Dorian Lynskey

First published 2008
by Aurum Press Ltd, 7 Greenland Street, London NW1 0ND
www.aurumpress.co.uk
in association with Guardian Books
Guardian Books is an imprint of Guardian Newspapers Ltd.

A catalogue record for this book is available from the
British Library.

ISBN 978 1 84513 317 7

10 9 8 7 6 5 4 3 2 1
2012 2011 2010 2009 2008

Text design: bluegumdesigners.com
Printed and bound by MPG Books, Bodmin, Cornwall

CONTENTS

INTRODUCTION

(▶) Once upon a time, not so long ago, there were mix tapes, and they were hard work. To craft the perfect compilation from a stack of CDs and vinyl required the forethought of a military strategist, the reflexes of a Formula One driver and the patience of a saint. I remember hunkering down by my dad's stereo with a pile of CDs, vinyl and tapes, fiddling with running orders and sound levels, dropping the needle on a record with one hand and swiftly releasing the tape deck's pause button with the other, working out the last possible moment that I could stop a song taped off the radio before the DJ's voice crashed in, cursing when I got it wrong, going over certain segues again and again, then carefully crafting a handmade sleeve and finally appraising the finished item. I couldn't have felt prouder if I had written every note myself.

A decent compilation tape was the work of an afternoon: an edifice that needed to be built from the ground up, brick by brick. Now there are playlists, which are infinitely easier. With iTunes, you can assemble a running order, correct any awkward segues, tinker to your heart's content and burn CDs for ten friends, all in less time than it takes to record a side of a C90. In a stroke, the tape seems as archaic as a telegram or a typewriter.

For anyone with a life to be getting on with, this must be a good thing, but there's no romance in convenience. The digital playlist sets the music fan a challenge: not simply to do an old job faster but to explore new possibilities.

Digital technology has had two major effects on the way we listen to music. First, it has usurped the rule of the album and replaced it with a democracy of individual tracks, from whatever source, in whatever order. The capacity for continued, practically effortless rearrangement allows songs to speak to each other across the genres and eras, to forge new connections based on surprising similarities. It lets you be more adventurous in your compilation-making.

Second, it has made the work of deciding *what* to listen to so much harder. When you can access thousands upon thousands of tracks from your desk in seconds, where do you begin? You know that your new favourite songs are out there, just waiting for you to find out about them. You have the transport but not the map. Even the music you already own becomes harder to navigate. It is not like gazing at a wall of CDs, waiting for one to trigger a visceral response: *Yes, this is the record I need to listen to right this minute.* When faced with an iPod laden with 10,000 tracks, your brain freezes. This, of course, is why the shuffle function exists, but randomness is only fitfully satisfying.

This book is a response to both of these new ways of listening. It began as a weekly column, called Readers Recommend, in the Friday edition of the *Guardian* in September 2005, from an idea by the section's editor, Merope Mills. Every week I set a theme on the paper's website and ask readers to suggest relevant songs. I then comb through the nominations, revisiting those I know and hunting down those I don't, before settling on a list of ten songs which are fun to discuss as well as to hear. Each playlist is accompanied by an essay discussing the inclusions and the logic behind them. It's like making a tape with a couple of hundred strangers offering advice over my shoulder, only with considerably less chance of blows being exchanged.

Week by week, I've watched the column attract a pool of regular recommenders as inquisitive, well-informed, witty and generous as I could have hoped for. To fulfil my end of the deal, I've had to be more open-minded than I have ever been in my life, listening to as many tracks as humanly possible, many from artists whom I've never previously given the time of day. I've discovered brand new passions – Tom Waits, Fela Kuti, Patti Smith, Magazine, old jazz standards, righteous 1970s reggae, early blues, folk-rock – and hoped that readers would find their own. Even then I couldn't find it in myself to like Sting, Cat Stevens, Steely Dan or the Red Hot Chili Peppers, but I'm only human.

The idea is not to establish a canonical list of the 'best' songs, because that drives you into the arms of received wisdom, where you end up relying on music which has already been well-travelled and approved by countless listeners before you. You get stuck on the highway, and that has many attractions – Beatlesburg, Dylanville, James Brown Town – but often the most interesting discoveries are hiding down the side roads. Many times I've left out an acknowledged classic to free up space for a neglected pearl.

The playlist titles are inevitably reductive: one of the joys of pop is that the meanings of songs are open to interpretation, and some of the best songs in the world are about nothing much at all. You may disagree with my readings of certain songs. Good. The idea is not to tell anyone what to think but to encourage closer listening, and to emphasise the infinite variety of the songwriter's art. Until I started this column, I had no idea how many songs I'd misunderstood by only hearing part of the lyric.

A meaty topic, whether it be war, or food, or loneliness, allows you to think laterally and cut across genres and time periods, seeing the diversity of songwriting but also the shared language. A rapper might have similar things to say about poverty to a blues musician who died years before the MC was born. A current indie-rock song might have a similar slant on heartbreak to a Motown classic. Willie Nelson and the Spice Girls might both have something useful to say about friendship. Listening to one kind of music, I sometimes find myself tuning out, but a wide-roaming playlist keeps me listening. I may not want to listen to a whole album by the 1920s black preacher Rev. A.W. Nix or 1980s soft-rock pin-up Belinda Carlisle but having them on the same playlist (Heaven and Hell) sharpens my enjoyment of both. I've tried not to patronise the reader by explaining who every artist is. If I've piqued your interest, there's this thing called the internet.

A digital playlist may have less romance than a tape but there's still an art to it. Each one in this book is carefully sequenced to be an enjoyable listening experience. You may notice that I like to start with something loud or odd and end on a slowie. Each one was enormous fun to make. Occasionally, like when it began to snow just as I was adding Galaxie 500's 'Listen, the Snow Is Falling' to the cold-themed list, it's been magical.

Neither book nor column would have come about if not for Merope Mills. I also have to thank her successor in the editor's chair, Michael Hann, and the regular recommenders from across the world over the past 32 months: AdamK, AlexaK, alexito, alicksboots, barbryn, BeltwayBandit, bethnoir, Blimpy McFlah, Bradley the Buyer, Carefree, CaroleBristol, Catcher, CraneSpire, Cyan, DarceysDad, Deviant, dominia, DrMaybe, earbud, ejaydee, ElDerino, englishhermit, fourfoot, frogprincess, GarethI, goneforeign, gordonimmel, ivorengine, Jamie77, jasonaparkes, Kalyr, kelley, Linsel, lonniej, Loumo, loyatemu, Luke the Drifter, Mainy, Mark68, Mnemonic, mototom, Mr DNA, MrMustard, murphsup, nilpferd, Paula, pdmalcolm, Proudfoot, raindog, richardrj, RockingMitch, samofnewcross, saneshane, scarymonster, Scribbler134, severin, ShivSidecar, simonbic, snadfrod, Steenbeck, suzi, SV80, SwissPhil, Tatanka Yotanka, tarxien, Tempusfugit, theboydaz, TheLetterO, TimnHazel, TonNL, tracyk, WKB1 and zoomusicgirl.

I suspect that only one person in the world will like every song in this book, but I hope you'll be inspired to try something new. I never trust anyone who asks me what kind of music I'm into – I'm sorely tempted to tell them I listen to nothing but bluegrass and booty bass – because any music fan with an inquiring mind and an internet connection should be into all kinds. The joy of the playlist is that it makes exploration easy. I'm not asking any reader to invest in a stack of krautrock or jazz albums. Just try the occasional unfamiliar song. See where it takes you. I'm ultimately just another listener, with his likes and dislikes, constantly searching for new songs to fall in love with. So argue with these playlists. Make your own, improved versions. A predictable, canonical list seals off debate with the dull stamp of certainty, but each of these lists aims to start a new conversation.

Oh, and one more thing about a ten-song playlist: it's roughly the same length as one side of a C90. Old habits die hard.

THE
PLAY

LISTS

ADOLESCENCE

▶ There is a scene of enormous, wordless poignancy in the film *Napoleon Dynamite*, in which Napoleon and his fellow sad sacks haunt the fringes of their high school prom while Alphaville's power ballad 'Forever Young' echoes around the hall. For them, you realise, to be forever young would constitute cruel and unusual punishment.

Thankfully, we're not all Napoleon Dynamite, but unless you happen to be that smirking twerp from Channel 4's *Skins*, chances are your adolescence isn't/wasn't a non-stop joyride. Teenagers are horny, insecure, idealistic, conflicted, self-righteous and self-loathing. They make for good music. Even the most exciting teenage songs have a tang of anxiety, whether it's the unsated desire in 'Teenage Kicks', or the dread shadow of daddy threatening to confiscate the T-Bird in 'Fun Fun Fun'.

You could argue that almost every song from rock 'n' roll's first decade was fundamentally about adolescence, vibrating with frustration at parental strictures and treating every romantic hiccup as if it were the end of the world. Dion and the Belmonts are maddened by hormones on 'A Teenager in Love's U-rated angst.

While the parents in 'C'mon Everybody' or 'Wouldn't It Be Nice' are implacable killjoys to be avoided rather than resisted, 'My Generation' hoists its middle finger at them. The Who fixated on adolescence long after they'd outgrown it, but never with such snotty zeal. Roger Daltrey stutters with indignation, mischievously telling his oppressors to f-f-f-f-fade away. He'd find common ground with smart-alec punks the Adverts, whose 'Bored Teenagers' is as eloquent as its title is blunt. Sonic Youth salute, and demonstrate, the cathartic force of a good, loud guitar in 'Teen Age Riot', a wonderfully improbable vision of mumbly Dinosaur Jr frontman J Mascis occupying the White House: 'You're never gonna stop all the teenage leather and booze.'

It's not all leather and booze, though. Nina Simone used the title of Lorraine Hansberry's unfinished play *To Be Young, Gifted and Black* to celebrate the potential of the post-civil rights generation whose adolescence was so much brighter than her own. I've chosen Bob and Marcia's reggae version. More bittersweet memories in 'When We Were Young' by Irish band Whipping Boy: 'When we were young nobody knew / Who you were or what you'd do / Nobody had a past that catches up on you.'

Seventeen is a potent age in pop: just think of Abba's untouchable dancing queen. Saturnine synth-poppers Ladytron breathe a cautionary word in her ear, reducing the desires of the fashion industry and lecherous older men to one taunting refrain: 'They only want you when you're seventeen / When you're twenty-one you're no fun.' To be undesirable even at seventeen means social oblivion for Janis Ian, sat at home 'inventing lovers on the phone' in a song just the right side of mawkish.

Sofia Coppola's *The Virgin Suicides* is a teen movie like no other: mysterious, erotic and exquisitely morbid. The characters communicate via classic rock but the deadly beauty of Air's theme tune evokes all that goes unsaid. Finally, Big Star's 'Thirteen' has an aching vulnerability that Brian Wilson or Frankie Lymon would have understood. 'Rock 'n' roll is here to stay' but adolescence, thankfully, passes.

THE PLAYLIST

A Teenager in Love Dion and the Belmonts
My Generation The Who
Bored Teenagers The Adverts
Teen Age Riot Sonic Youth
To Be Young, Gifted and Black Bob and Marcia
When We Were Young Whipping Boy
Seventeen Ladytron
At Seventeen Janis Ian
Playground Love Air
Thirteen Big Star

AUTUMN

(▶) I'm not one of those fusty, letter-writing Little Englanders who seem to regard the very existence of American English as a dashed impertinence, but I've never understood the logic behind renaming a season *fall*. It sounds so bluntly prosaic compared to the ripely evocative *autumn*.

Because autumn songs tend towards the wistful, sorrowful souls with acoustic guitars are in their element. It would be easy to compile a playlist consisting only of Nick Drake, Van Morrison and Nico, or simply play the entirety of *Out of Season*, Beth Gibbons and Rustin Man's impeccably autumnal 2002 album, but there's a limit to how many sombre ruminations a person can handle.

Kurt Weill's 'September Song' is one of the great standards, performed by Lou Reed, Ian McCulloch and Ella Fitzgerald among others, but Sinatra's faultless rendition does it for me. The strings swirl around him like leaves in the wind. There's a biting chill to the I-miss-you sentiments of 'Dead Leaves and the Dirty Ground' by the White Stripes: not so much melancholy as scorched-earth melodrama.

For all its apparent jollity, the Kinks' 'Autumn Almanac' evokes the humdrum minutiae of English life as deftly as anything else in Ray Davies's songbook: 'Tea and toasted, buttered currant buns / Can't compensate for lack of sun.' The Small Faces' days were growing short when they recorded the exquisitely sad and weary 'The Autumn Stone', shaded red and gold. The departure of songwriter Steve Marriott before it was released made it all the more elegiac.

More quintessential Englishness from Fairport Convention, whose 'Who Knows Where the Time Goes' is one of the most beautiful songs in the world: birds fly south, winter beckons and Sandy Denny curls up by the fire. A less widely recognised folk singer, Vashti Bunyan, released her second album in 2005 after a thirty-five-year hiatus. From her debut, 'Rose Hip November' is an exquisite, ethereal hymn to the change of seasons. You can practically smell the woodsmoke.

New Jersey's Yo La Tengo are the kind of critically adored alt-rock toilers who release album after album with scant hope of a commercial breakthrough. 'Autumn Sweater' should have done the trick, with its lolloping, quasi-baggy breakbeat and tender vocals. Strange Anglo-American title though – shouldn't it be either Fall Sweater or Autumn Jumper? Moving on, Abba's popularity with hen nights and Alan Partridge has somewhat obscured their talent for melancholy, but 'When All Is Said and Done' is a deliciously bittersweet break-up song, full of sanguine reflections on the quartet's recent divorces: 'When the summer's over and the dark clouds hide the sun / Neither you nor I'm to blame when all is said and done.'

'Autumn Leaves' is another standard, made famous by Edith Piaf and reworked for the comedown generation by Coldcut. A thousand

Ibiza chillout compilations cannot wither the yearning ambience of the Irresistible Force remix. In REM's piano ballad 'Nightswimming', summer's fading, 'September's coming soon', and every note is suffused with a distinctly autumnal glow: an indefinable sense of loss and longing.

THE PLAYLIST

September Song Frank Sinatra
Dead Leaves and the Dirty Ground The White Stripes
Autumn Almanac The Kinks
The Autumn Stone The Small Faces
Who Knows Where the Time Goes Fairport Convention
Rose Hip November Vashti Bunyan
Autumn Sweater Yo La Tengo
When All Is Said and Done Abba
Autumn Leaves (Irresistible Force remix) Coldcut
Nightswimming REM

SONGS ABOUT
WEEKENDS

(▶) It's over fifty years since Little Richard whooped, 'Well it's Saturday night and I just got paid!' on 'Rip It Up'. Flexi-time and automated bank transfers may have diluted its magic, but the weekend song endures. On one level, pop will never stop being about getting stupid when the working week ends, and thank God for that.

A good weekend record requires empathy. For all its musical virtues, Flowered Up's 'Weekender' is fundamentally the unsavoury sound of a rave-scene insider sneering at ordinary working schmoes, and Paul Weller is at his most dourly patronising on the Jam's 'Saturday's Kids'. Shopgirls drinking Babycham? Heaven forbid. No wonder the Arctic Monkeys' open-minded everyday vignettes have proved so popular with those who think their lifestyles merit neither pity nor contempt.

Like so many weekend songs, the Easybeats' 1967 psych-pop hit 'Friday On My Mind' works its way through all the drabber days ('Monday morning feels so bad . . .') before exploding into the one that matters. Norma Jean works a similar trick on the unutterably joyful, Chic-produced 'Saturday': 'I just can't wait till Saturday!' Disco's escapist manifesto made some kind of reference to nine-to-five drudgery practically compulsory – Michael Jackson's *Off the Wall* is almost a concept album on the theme. Richard and Linda Thompson invest the idea with a distinctly British absence of glamour: 'A couple of drunken nights rolling on the floor / Is just the kind of mess I'm looking for.' You wouldn't catch Norma Jean doing that.

Muting his misanthropy for once, Arab Strap's Aidan Moffat warmly details the first big weekend of a 1990s Glasgow summer, from club to flat to park to pub. Specific yet universal, it takes me back to my mid-twenties like nothing else. Meanwhile in 1940s New Orleans, Louis Jordan spins his own antic yarn about a rough night out, ending with the grumpy instruction, 'Don't ever mention a fish to me!' Safer, it seems, to strap on a pair of skates with a jubilant De La Soul.

But what about those excluded from the pill-popping, fish-frying, roller-skating jamboree? Cue the Cure's '10:15 Saturday Night'. Like a post-punk précis of Roman Polanski's *Repulsion*, it magnifies simple loneliness into full-blown psychosis. Even the narrator's flat has turned against him: the tap drips, the clock ticks, the drumsticks click-click-click-click. The Specials' Terry Hall fares a little better. I'm not sure anyone will ever top this representation of an average British night out: the deadpan observations, the eerie funhouse organ, Hall's Eeyoreish delivery and that perfect closing couplet, 'Wish I had lipstick on my shirt / Instead of piss stains on my shoes.' Did he have fun? He's not sure.

From one smeary dawn to another. All of Tom Waits's *The Heart of Saturday Night* album, with its cast of swaying nighthawks, would be suitable. The title track's a beauty but the scenario painted in the final one – hash browns, eggs and cigarettes as the sun comes up – fits our tired and emotional mood better. Finally, Nick Drake eases us into a melancholy Sunday so gently that even booze-battered brains won't protest.

THE PLAYLIST

Friday on My Mind The Easybeats

Saturday Norma Jean

I Want to See the Bright Lights Richard and Linda Thompson

The First Big Weekend Arab Strap

Saturday Night Fish Fry Louis Jordan and his Tympany Five

A Roller Skating Jam Named 'Saturdays' De La Soul

10:15 Saturday Night The Cure

Friday Night, Saturday Morning The Specials

The Ghosts of Saturday Night (After Hours at Napoleone's Pizza House) Tom Waits

Saturday Sun Nick Drake

SONGS ABOUT
BEING ALONE

▶ Novelist Jonathan Franzen titled his 2002 volume of essays after a skill that he believes is harder than it seems: *How to Be Alone*. It is a lesson that pop has never really learned – in fact, it's probably part of the 'noisy and distracting mass culture' Franzen complains about. Pop's defining concerns are love, dancing and other activities which require company, so to be alone, whether it's Sam Cooke in 'Another Saturday Night' or Morrissey in 'How Soon Is Now?', is somehow to have failed.

Certainly, that's what I found when considering the possibilities for this playlist: hundreds of break-up songs, of varying degrees of eloquence (can Otis Redding's 'this loneliness won't leave me alone' be beaten?), and only a handful which, like the Beach Boys' 'In My Room', contend that there are benefits to solitude.

In 'Tower of Song', Leonard Cohen claims to have 'said to Hank Williams, how lonely does it get?' Hank's answer, one imagines after hearing 'I'm So Lonesome I Could Cry', is 'very'. That wonderful Americanism, *lonesome*, and the references to far-off train whistles and bird calls, suggest that the sheer size of America is conspiring against him. The Secret Machines' Brandon Curtis also wonders where his woman is, with a touch of self-mockery, on the magnificent 'Alone, Jealous and Stoned'.

'Alone Again Or' is the perfect opening to Love's troubling 1967 masterpiece *Forever Changes*: musically seductive (that glorious trumpet solo) yet lyrically estranging. When the zeitgeist cried 'Come together!', they stood apart. 'Alive Alone' also swims against the tide, with lyrics written, surprisingly, not by guest singer Beth Orton but by Chemical Brother Tom Rowlands. Surely dance music, that most communal of genres, has never produced another couplet as desolate as: 'I'm alive and I'm alone / And I never wanted to be either of those.'

And so to the long-term lonely. Stax one-hit wonder Frederick Knight broadcasts his despair from his too-large bed, while Abba detail a loner's daily routine with deadly precision: the vexing newspaper editorial, the episodes of *Dallas*, the Chinese takeaway, that seventh cigarette. Who exactly disrupted that routine (a lover? A killer? Death?) is left ominously vague. 'It's funny, but I had no sense of living without aim / The day before you came.'

From Slick Rick, the rapper who once recorded 'Treat Her Like a Prostitute', 'All Alone (No One to Be With)' is a revelation: a haunting, sensitive narrative of a woman who always draws the short straw. Gang of Four's *Heart of Darkness*-quoting 'We Live As We Dream, Alone' is protest music with the fight knocked out of it. The system has beaten them: 'Everybody is in too many pieces.'

At last, an upbeat perspective. For Suzanne Vega, solitude is a mysterious protecting spirit who appears sporadically 'to set a twisted thing straight'. And here's Rufus Wainwright, covering his father

Loudon's 'One Man Guy', a wittier account of wilful isolation than Simon and Garfunkel's 'I Am a Rock': 'These three cubic feet of bone and blood and meat are all I love and know.' Sister Martha provides harmonies, so he isn't alone at all. Nice touch.

THE PLAYLIST

I'm So Lonesome I Could Cry Hank Williams

Alone, Jealous and Stoned The Secret Machines

Alone Again Or Love

Alive Alone The Chemical Brothers

I've Been Lonely For So Long Frederick Knight

The Day Before You Came Abba

All Alone (No One to Be With) Slick Rick

We Live As We Dream, Alone Gang of Four

Solitude Standing Suzanne Vega

One Man Guy Rufus Wainwright

HATCHET JOBS

(▶) We all lose our temper and say things we regret but few of us get the opportunity to record them for posterity, which is probably for the best. Graham Coxon's 'Song for the Sick' is a petulant squib that would embarrass somebody half his age, and 'Get in the Ring' by Guns 'n' Roses is the pathetic sound of brattish megastars naming and shaming hostile critics. Several splenetic break-up songs, meanwhile, simply reek of misogyny. Honourable mention goes to Nick Cave's legendary B-side 'Scum', though. It may be a petty assault on an erstwhile flatmate but the insults are compellingly lurid: 'He reminded me of some evil gnome / Shaking hands was like shaking a hot, fat, oily bone.' Ew.

Nothing tops Shellac's 'Prayer to God' for sheer malevolence. Frontman Steve Albini requests the immediate smiting of his ex ('she can go quietly', he allows) and her new boyfriend, yet seems to acknowledge how desperate and impotent his murderous fantasies are. Redressing the gender balance is Kelis's astounding, genre-subverting debut single: in an R'n'B context, the chorus's scream of frustration detonates like an emotional nailbomb.

These days 2Pac is rap's soulful saint, duetting with Sir Elton from beyond the grave, but 'Hit 'Em Up', recorded during the mid-'90s hip-hop wars, reminds us what a spectacular bastard he could be.

During the course of this assault on the entire eastern seaboard, he claims to have slept with Notorious BIG's wife and mocks another rival rapper for having sickle-cell anaemia. It's at once breathtaking and utterly repellent. Rock's equivalent in the reputation-souring stakes is 'How Do You Sleep?', John and Yoko's infamous evisceration of Paul McCartney.

Loudon Wainwright III holds the rare distinction of being attacked on disc by both his children: Rufus with 'Dinner at Eight' and Martha with 'Bloody Mother Fucking Asshole'. Martha's song is emotion with the skin peeled back, red and raw. With a withering sneer as his default setting, this theme is Bob Dylan's forte, but 'Positively 4th Street' beats the rest thanks to a jaunty Trojan-horse melody which smuggled the backbiting politics of the Greenwich Village folk scene into one of his biggest hits.

The Dead Kennedys' 1979 punk satire gave California's Democratic governor Jerry Brown a somewhat unjust reputation as a New Age fascist. Updating it thirteen years later, Disposable Heroes of Hiphoprisy focused the song's ire on Republican incumbent Pete Wilson; surely a Schwarzenegger version is overdue. Britpop's romantic entanglements produced no song more mellifluously damning than Justine Frischmann's look back at life with Suede's Brett Anderson: 'You were far too busy writing rhymes that didn't scan.'

Obliged by his divorce settlement to pay all the royalties from his next album to ex-wife Anna Gordy, Marvin Gaye devoted the whole of *Here, My Dear* to demolishing her. This pivotal track sounds like razor-blades dipped in honey. In the ranks of songwriters' *bêtes noires*, Margaret Thatcher looms larger than most. Elvis Costello's viciously eloquent character assassination is one of the few hatchet jobs to make you think more of the author, not less.

THE PLAYLIST

Prayer to God Shellac
Caught Out There Kelis
Hit 'Em Up 2Pac
How Do You Sleep? John Lennon
Bloody Mother Fucking Asshole Martha Wainwright
Positively 4th Street Bob Dylan
California Über Alles The Dead Kennedys
Never Here Elastica
When Did You Stop Loving Me, When Did I Stop Loving You
  Marvin Gaye
Tramp the Dirt Down Elvis Costello

SONGS ABOUT
RAIN

▶ Like English commuters making stilted conversation, or horror film directors in want of a dramatic denouement, songwriters can't resist the allure of lousy weather. Rain is the metaphor that keeps on giving: it can stand, equally successfully, for heartache or war or joyous catharsis. And it's a fine excuse to get out the old sound effects records. *Cracka-boom! Kazam!* And so on.

Providing the calm before the storm, the disconsolate Temptations commence the playlist praying for the weather to match their mood. Eventually you hear the crash of a cloudburst, but it's dwarfed by the opening of Nick Cave's 'Tupelo', which sounds as if someone has dynamited the sky. Cave is in full Old Testament flow here, portending an almighty deluge while drummer Mick Harvey supplies the thunder. I would pay good money to see Cave present the weather on TV. 'Lookee *yonn-derrr!*' he'd cry, gesturing towards a low-pressure area approaching from the Atlantic. 'A big black cloud come! The beast it cometh down!'

Through the wonder of the iTunes fade function, Cave's downpour mutates into that of Phil Spector. The Ronettes make the prospect of taking a stroll in a downpour sound infinitely more tempting than it ever does in real life. You certainly wouldn't want to take a walk in Nick Cave's rain; you'd probably die. More buoyant sentiments from the Jesus and Mary Chain at their pop peak, and the Pogues, whose 'Rainy Night in Soho' feels like finding solace in a warm pub on a damp night.

After that bout of waterlogged exuberance, spirits sink again on Creedence Clearwater Revival's 'Have You Ever Seen the Rain?', an oblique, haunting protest song written in the wake of Altamont, Charles Manson and the Kent State shootings. One classic song samples another, as Missy Elliott uses Ann Peebles's 1974 soul hit 'I Can't Stand the Rain' to gripping effect on the narcoleptic funk of her debut single; the raindrop-simulating plink-plonk strings are joined by the sound of distant thunder.

Hard to say which is the best rendition of the 1933 song used a decade later as the theme for the musical *Stormy Weather*, the benchmark for pathetic fallacy songs in which the climate outside mirrors emotions inside. I love the earthy richness of Etta James's voice; you might prefer Lena Horne or Frank Sinatra. Randy Newman's quietly devastating account of the great Mississippi flood of 1927 is sung here by Aaron Neville. It's not just Neville's superior voice but the fact that, as a son of New Orleans, he performed it on US TV following 2005's inundation, thus demonstrating how little had changed. Just replace Evangeline with New Orleans and Coolidge with Bush.

Finally, back to Britain for Blur's 'This Is a Low', arguably Britpop's fullest achievement. Damon Albarn finesses the accidental poetry of the shipping forecast into a meteorological metaphor for England's troubled psyche, while Graham Coxon unfurls his billowing guitar solo as if he's standing on Beachy Head in the middle of a gale. And now over to Nick Cave, with the weather.

THE PLAYLIST

I Wish It Would Rain The Temptations

Tupelo Nick Cave and the Bad Seeds

Walking in the Rain The Ronettes

Happy When It Rains The Jesus and Mary Chain

A Rainy Night in Soho The Pogues

Have You Ever Seen the Rain? Creedence Clearwater Revival

The Rain (Supa Dupa Fly) Missy 'Misdemeanour' Elliott

Stormy Weather Etta James

Louisiana 1927 Aaron Neville

This Is a Low Blur

CELEBRITY

(▶) Orthodoxy dictates that no worthwhile musician should ever admit to enjoying fame; that on one hand there are starry-eyed wannabes who would gargle cat sick if it would guarantee them an appearance in *Heat* magazine, and on the other there are noble artists with a monkish disdain for the trappings of celebrity; that you're either Kerry Katona or Captain Beefheart.

It's nonsense, of course. Most major musicians exist somewhere in between, playing the game when it suits them and scorning it when it doesn't. Hence most potshots at celebrity, from the Byrds' 'So You Want To Be A Rock 'n' Roll Star' to Nine Inch Nails' 'Starfuckers, Inc.', are either bitter, facile or hypocritical, if not all three. Great songs about celebrity demand something more than a condescending sneer.

So it's good to start with the unapologetic hunger of Oasis's self-fulfilling prophecy 'Rock 'n' Roll Star'. To hear it performed live fourteen years on, it's practically meaningless, a statement of mundane fact, but think back to when Noel Gallagher wrote it, musing not on fame but on how it feels to be young and fearless, and it still sets the neck hairs prickling.

Courtney Love's notoriety is so vast and voracious that she can barely write about anything else. 'Celebrity Skin' was her last truly great song, a smart and snappy Hollywood anthem. Rachel Stevens's 'Some Girls' is wonderful self-questioning pop. The former S Club 7 singer's debut solo single had stalled at number two when Richard X and Hannah Robinson composed this electro-glam stunner about a frustrated starlet whose 'dreams of number one last forever'. Naturally, it stalled at number two.

Pet Shop Boys wrote 'Shameless' back in 1994, which in retrospect seems like some golden age of humility, and it becomes more pertinent with every year. This brash, hi-NRG show tune, which grudgingly admires gimlet-eyed ambition even as it mocks it, could be the opening number in X-Factor: the Musical: 'We have no integrity, we're ready to crawl / To obtain celebrity, we'll do anything at all.' Bowie's icy, anhedonic 'Fame' would fit but I prefer the flash and fizz of 'Star' – another song you could build a musical around.

Loretta Lynn counts the cost of her partner's newfound fame ('Success has made a failure of our home'), while 'Deception', by west coast rappers Blackalicious, is another cautionary tale about an overnight sensation who behaves so abominably that he ends up back at the bottom, *sans* friends. 'Paint a Vulgar Picture' is a damning portrait of record label cynicism but the fact that Morrissey, for all his protestations, so obviously craves stardom makes the pivotal line – 'You could have walked away . . . couldn't you?' – deliciously bittersweet.

Finally, two reflections on old-school celebrity. On 'New Age', the Velvet Underground visit a faded star and her obsessive young fan; on the grand and moving 'Celluloid Heroes', Ray Davies takes a morbid stroll down Hollywood Boulevard. As a film critic, Davies is no David Thomson – every male actor here is a stereotype and every female one a tragic crack-up – but we can forgive him that.

THE PLAYLIST

Rock 'n' Roll Star Oasis
Celebrity Skin Hole
Some Girls Rachel Stevens
Shameless Pet Shop Boys
Star David Bowie
Success Loretta Lynn
Deception Blackalicious
Paint a Vulgar Picture The Smiths
New Age The Velvet Underground
Celluloid Heroes The Kinks

PROTEST
SONHS

SONGS

▶ In 2007, an interviewer from music website Pitchfork asked Jack White, 'When people mix pop and politics, it can so easily fall on its face, can't it?' 'Yeah,' replied White, 'that or it can start a riot. One or the other.' The history of protest songs is one of extremes: whip-smart or dumb as rocks, generous or pompous, powerful enough to change the world or just so much hot air. Some of the dullest, smuggest, preachiest songs in the world have a political message, and so do some of the very best. No other subject is a greater test of a songwriter's art.

The opening troika speaks for three generations of black America. Back in 1939, Billie Holiday recorded arguably the first modern protest song, written by Jewish schoolteacher Abel Meeropol about lynchings in the Deep South; the strange fruit are 'black bodies swinging in the breeze'. *Time* magazine denounced it as 'a prime piece of musical propaganda', so it must have been doing something right. A quarter-century on, not enough had changed and Sam Cooke, spurred into action by Bob Dylan's 'Blowin' in the Wind', intertwined the personal and political on 'A Change Is Gonna Come', a song whose bruised nobility spoke for millions of Americans. And twenty-five years after *that* came 'Fight the Power' from hip-hop's most thrilling polemicists. It's technically about African-Americans appreciating their history but whatever power you happen to be fighting, this militantly funky rallying cry fits the bill.

In 1979, Stiff Little Fingers were briefly hailed as Belfast's answer to the Clash thanks to 'Alternative Ulster', their bracingly stroppy demand for a Troubles-free life. The 1965 Watts riots prompted Frank Zappa to pen the apocalyptic psychedelia of 'Trouble Every Day', which aims its withering contempt at the police, the mobs and the media alike. Zappa's invitation to 'take your TV tube and eat it' segues nicely into the Disposable Heroes of Hiphoprisy's hip-hop homage to Gil Scott-Heron's 'The Revolution Will Not Be Televised', with its channel-surfing blitz of samples.

Under some regimes, a protest song can land you in jail, or worse. Recorded by Fela Kuti in 1976, 'Zombie's hypnotic funk poked fun at the Nigerian army's thuggish drones. When the song caught on, the thuggish drones retaliated by beating Fela, burning down his commune and mortally wounding his mother. Most political bands have to contend with nothing more hurtful than bad reviews. Elsewhere in Africa, apartheid inspired its own fertile pop subgenre. The Special AKA's 'Nelson Mandela' put the imprisoned ANC leader's name on the lips of every British schoolchild.

Some protest songs don't waste any time. Eleven days after the National Guard killed four student demonstrators at Kent State University, Neil Young wrote and recorded his angry response, with its damning mantra, 'Four dead in Ohio'. Finally, something to represent the resurgence in political songwriting fuelled by contempt for George W Bush. Asking 'Do you remember the forgotten America?', Willy Mason's eloquent 'Oxygen' captures the tenor of the times: jaded, frustrated, confused, yet cautiously optimistic.

THE PLAYLIST

Strange Fruit Billie Holiday
A Change Is Gonna Come Sam Cooke
Fight the Power Public Enemy
Alternative Ulster Stiff Little Fingers
Trouble Every Day Frank Zappa and the Mothers of Invention
Television, the Drug of the Nation Disposable Heroes of
   Hiphoprisy
Zombie Fela Kuti and Afrika 70
Nelson Mandela The Special AKA
Ohio Crosby, Stills, Nash and Young
Oxygen Willy Mason

SCARY
SONGS

(▶) When you hear a piece of music which unnerves you, it's worth asking why. Is it the subject matter? A certain noise? Something indefinable in the voice? Scary music comes in many forms, from Nico's mausoleum moan to Tricky's claustrophobic growl, Current 93's ambient shivers to Jandek's Blair Witch blues, the woman-scorned rage of P.J. Harvey's 'Rid of Me' to the infernal psychedelia of the Cure's 'Pornography'. This playlist features the kind of song you'd think twice about listening to alone on a long dark night, the kind that creeps into your bones.

Throbbing Gristle's 'Hamburger Lady' seeps out of the speakers like an infection. A distorted voice ghoulishly describes a burns victim as unidentifiably harrowing noises drift in and out of earshot and an electronic drone lifts and drops like a cold wind. Brrr. After that, Suicide's 'Frankie Teardrop', the Springsteen-in-hell story of a struggling factory worker who murders his family, almost qualifies as comic relief. Watch out for the screams though.

Hearing 'The Boiler' twenty-five years after it came out, it seems inconceivable that it was ever a Top 40 hit. One can only imagine the reaction of Specials fans to Rhoda Dakar's distressing account of a date gone horribly wrong. It makes 'Ghost Town' sound like 'Agadoo'. The very best gangsta rap is attuned to the moral consequences of the bloodshed it describes. Backed by an *Omen*-style choir, the Wu-Tang Clan's Genius/GZA climbs inside the head of a drug dealer corroded by violence: 'Under the subway, waiting for the train to make noise / So I can blast a nigga and his boys – for what?'

From *Bitches Brew* forward, Miles Davis seemed intent on scaring away those lightweights who liked to play *Kind of Blue* over dinner. On 1972's 'Rated X', Miles and his band play like they hate each other, not to mention everyone else, the discordant organ ramping up the tension while the guitars churn evilly below. Suffice to say it would put anyone off their soup.

Few albums have as fearsome a reputation as Scott Walker's *Tilt*, on which the one-time MOR pin-up plunged headlong into the heart of darkness. 'The Cockfighter' intersperses lyrics taken from the trial of Adolf Eichmann with the clanking of heavy machinery. Nothing will send unwanted house guests scrambling for the door quicker, unless it's the Manic Street Preachers' aptly titled 'The Intense Humming of Evil'. Inspired by a visit to Auschwitz, it's the sound of moral disgust souring into outright misanthropy.

'In a Lonely Place' was one of the last songs Joy Division's Ian Curtis wrote before hanging himself. Afterwards, his old bandmates recorded it and the song entered a whole new dimension of bleakness: half suicide note, half funeral march. Nick Drake's own youthful demise retrospectively made the eerie 'Black Eyed Dog' sound like a premonition of death. Finally, Blind Willie Johnson condenses all human misery into a wordless, fathomless moan which sucks all the light out of the room. As they used to say on *Crimewatch*: don't have nightmares.

THE PLAYLIST

Hamburger Lady Throbbing Gristle
Frankie Teardrop Suicide
The Boiler The Special AKA and Rhoda Dakar
Gold Genius/GZA
Rated X Miles Davis
The Cockfighter Scott Walker
The Intense Humming of Evil Manic Street Preachers
In a Lonely Place New Order
Black Eyed Dog Nick Drake
Dark Was the Night, Cold Was the Ground Blind Willie
    Johnson

SONGS REDEFINED BY
MOVIES

(▶) Never underestimate the power of an underexposed song, intelligently chosen. Skilled directors turn songs inside out, tapping previously unglimpsed potential, while lazy ones just ask pop music to do the emotional heavy lifting for them. Dragooned into the last scene of *Love Actually*, 'God Only Knows' contains more genuine feeling in three minutes than the rest of Richard Curtis's rotten schmaltzfest put together.

Alas, no room in the final ten for such expert selectors as Scorsese, Wes Anderson, John Hughes or Wong Kar-Wai. And no *Garden State* because the moment when winsome indie-girl Natalie Portman earnestly insists 'The Shins will change your life' makes me hate the Shins, Natalie Portman and life itself.

We begin, aptly, with two opening scenes. Without the napalm and a demented Martin Sheen, 'The End' is a thick slice of overcooked ham; with them, it's the sound of creeping insanity. Just as that song has become musical shorthand for Vietnam, Gershwin's 'Rhapsody in Blue' will always represent an idealised New York, thanks to Woody Allen.

Good films can give neglected songs an Indian summer of popularity. *The Big Lebowski* introduced audiences to Kenny Rogers's long-forgotten jaunt on the psychedelia bandwagon, while *Reservoir Dogs* reinvented Stealer's Wheel's deeply unfashionable 1970s soft-rock. With its confluence of black comedy, pop ephemera and shocking violence, Mr Blonde's torture-cum-dance scene is Tarantino's aesthetic in a nutshell. Arguably, *American Psycho*'s Huey Lewis-soundtracked carnage is wittier but I can't quite bring myself to include 'Hip to Be Square'.

David Lynch often reveals more through music than through dialogue, and Blue Velvet's theme of corrupted innocence reaches full bloom when a lip-synching Dean Stockwell slithers inside Roy Orbison's 'In Dreams'. Moving from lip-synching to karaoke, Bill Murray's lugubrious rendition of Roxy Music's 'More Than This' is a hidden track on the *Lost in Translation* soundtrack. The song, like the film, is all about things transient and elusive: 'fallen leaves in the night'.

If it's hard to ruin a great song (unless you're Richard Curtis), then it's harder still to rescue a supposedly naff one. The climactic dance scene in *Napoleon Dynamite* vindicates not just the geeky anti-hero but also his song of choice, revealing that beneath Jamiroquai's twattish millinery, 'Canned Heat' is a latter-day disco classic. Similarly, Cameron Crowe helped make Elton John hip. In *Almost Famous*, this old track about groupies (and not, as I initially thought, an ode to US sitcom actor Tony Danza) unites the squabbling, inarticulate musicians in a cathartic singalong.

Finally, two endings. When Rupert Murdoch first saw how *Fight Club*'s climax played terrorism for laughs and romance, he was apparently incensed by what his Twentieth Century Fox executives had green-lit, an image which makes the Pixies' 'Where Is My Mind?' all the more enjoyable. The sour irony of *Dr Strangelove*'s apocalyptic denouement was even more controversial in its day. Vera Lynn's wartime pick-me-up was never quite the same again.

THE PLAYLIST

The End The Doors
Rhapsody in Blue George Gershwin
Just Dropped In (To See What Condition My Condition Was In) Kenny Rogers and the First Edition
Stuck in the Middle with You Stealer's Wheel
In Dreams Roy Orbison
More Than This Bill Murray
Canned Heat Jamiroquai
Tiny Dancer Elton John
Where Is My Mind? Pixies
We'll Meet Again Vera Lynn

DANCING

(▶) In pop music, there is dancing and there is 'dancing'. I still remember the jolt when I realised, rather tardily, that Madonna's 'Into the Groove' was not all it seemed. Why else would she be 'tired of dancing here all by myself'? Or is that just me? This list features only the kind of dancing you can do in public.

We hit the dancefloor running with Deee-Lite's irresistible invitation to 'dance and have some fun'. This acid-disco evergreen is every DJ's break-glass-in-case-of-emergency record; if you can't move to this, then seek medical help. Then it's all twelve glorious minutes of Sly and the Family Stone's 'Dance to the Medley'. A constantly mutating, effects-heavy director's cut of their 1968 hit 'Dance to the Music', it pushed funk music into far-flung psychedelic realms.

There were so many dance crazes in the late 1950s and early '60s that only a list record could reflect them all. Cue Ray Charles's raucous catalogue of briefly popular moves, from the watusi to the mashed potato. Roxy Music later gave the idea an arch, elitist twist, offering a new sensation for those 'bored of the beguine'. If anyone out there knows exactly how one does the strand, do let me know.

In 1971, singer-songwriter Laura Nyro teamed up with future disco stars Labelle and producers Gamble and Huff for *Gonna Take a Miracle*, a collection of soul covers. Here they segue from Major Lance's 'Monkey Time' into a loose, funky reading of Martha and the Vandellas' 'Dancing in the Street' which is preferable to Jagger and Bowie's 1985 version on account of not making me want to saw my own head off with embarrassment.

Whereas many subsequent indie bands looked askance at both dancing and the radio (The Smiths' 'Panic' springs to mind), Joy Division's Ian Curtis portrays them on 'Transmission' as the purest of pleasures – 'no language, just sound, that's all we need know' – before exploding into a desperately urgent cry of 'dance dance dance dance dance to the radio'. The politicised punk-funk of Joy Division contemporaries Gang of Four inspired Radio 4's riposte to Rudy Giuliani's NY clubbing crackdown; remixer Trevor Jackson ramps up the militant clamour. Then Fatboy Slim's 'Body Movin' remix finds two expert purveyors of big, dumb party music at their biggest and dumbest; it bustles with life.

The last dance goes to the Drifters' tired and emotional end-of-night plea but if I could only choose one it would be Chic's 'Everybody Dance', the first thing that disco's dream team ever wrote together. The key line, 'The good times always end too soon', provides the tang of poignancy that sharpens the joy in all the best disco. If there's a philosophy to dance songs it's this: have fun while you can because nothing lasts for ever. Or, as Madonna sang on 'Into the Groove', 'I hope this feeling never ends tonight.' But then we know what she was getting at.

THE PLAYLIST

Groove Is in the Heart Deee-Lite
Dance to the Medley Sly and the Family Stone
Shake a Tail Feather Ray Charles
Do the Strand Roxy Music
Monkey Time / Dancing in the Street Laura Nyro and Labelle
Transmission Joy Division
Dance to the Underground (Playgroup remix) Radio 4
Body Movin' (Fatboy Slim remix) Beastie Boys
Everybody Dance (12" mix) Chic
Save the Last Dance for Me The Drifters

SMOKING

The first time I heard 'A Day in the Life', what surprised me most wasn't the radical structure or George Martin's vertiginous orchestration; it was Paul McCartney's line about smoking on the bus. You could smoke on buses back then? It seemed so improbably distant. Perhaps thirty years from now the cigarette will go virtually unmentioned in pop music and an arthritic Oasis will rename their Britpop singalong 'Salted Nuts and Alcohol'.

For now, though, it's one of music's hardest-working metaphors, standing for companionship in Simon and Garfunkel's 'America' ('We smoked the last one an hour ago'), carefree youth in Supergrass's 'Alright' ('Smoke a fag, put it out'), betrayal in Pet Shop Boys' 'So Hard' ('We've both given up smoking, 'cause it's fatal, so whose matches are those?') and life itself in Bowie's 'Rock 'n' Roll Suicide' ('Time takes a cigarette, puts it in your mouth'). And sometimes, as Freud almost said, a cigarette is just a cigarette.

References to more pungent combustibles tend towards the prosaic. It seems that all the ingenuity has gone into inventing new euphemisms rather than finessing them into poetry. The gist of most marijuana songs is: (a) don't bogart that joint, (b) pass the dutchie 'pon the left-hand side (see (a)) and (c) legalise it (don't criticise it).

So it's a playlist of two halves. Before the US criminalised marijuana, there was a fertile genre known as reefer jazz, of which Ella Fitzgerald's 'When I Get Low I Get High' is an exuberant example. Sixty years later, hip-hop picked up the baton. Setting aside Snoop Dogg and Cypress Hill, I've chosen this boisterous 1992 offering from Redman because it's not just underrated; it's educational too. Similarly, choosing just one reggae song is a tall order, but U-Roy's 'Chalice in the Palace' is surely the most novel. Inspired by a dream, he sketches out his plan to bond with the Queen over a hashpipe. Arise, Sir U-Roy.

Tonight's the Night was Neil Young's most ragged and inebriated album. This bleary-eyed country-rocker, looking back at Woodstock through a fog of smoke and regret, strongly suggests that Young took the Method approach during its recording. Super Furry Animals' rambling, rousing 'Smokin' is a prime slice of Rizla philosophy which rhymes 'meaning of life' with 'Johann Cruyff'.

And so to regular cigarettes. For Hefner's Darren Hayman, at his most biting and infectious here, they're the equivalent of Proust's madeleines: 'Camel Lights remind me of my ex-girlfriend at Christmas time / And Marlboro Reds remind me of giving up in Berlin.' For Rufus Wainwright on this charismatic 2001 show tune, they're emblematic of his self-destructive habits. Cigars rarely figure in pop but Serge Gainsbourg and Catherine Deneuve speak up for stogie fans by contending that God smokes them. Don't ask me, I'm no theologian.

Finally, two songs from an era before health warnings. Paired with coffee by Otis Redding, they're fuel for two infatuated lovers talking late into the night. Smouldering in Patsy Cline's ashtray, they're potent emblems of a devastating affair. Neither would work quite as well with salted nuts.

THE PLAYLIST

When I Get Low I Get High Ella Fitzgerald

How to Roll a Blunt Redman

Chalice in the Palace U-Roy

Roll Another Number (for the Road) Neil Young

Smokin' Super Furry Animals

The Hymn for the Cigarettes Hefner

Cigarettes and Chocolate Milk Rufus Wainwright

Dieu Fumeur des Havanes Serge Gainsbourg and Catherine Deneuve

Cigarettes and Coffee Otis Redding

Three Cigarettes in an Ashtray Patsy Cline

SONGS ABOUT
DRINKING

(▶) When you write a song that prominently features alcohol it doesn't matter what it's actually about: you're doomed to appear on albums with titles like *The Best Pissed Up Party Anthems Ever*. Underworld's 'Born Slippy', a troubled, impressionistic account of a heavy night out, has become simply the 'lager, lager, lager, lager' song, while thick-necked men in football shirts don't necessarily savour the bitter irony of 'we don't talk about love, we only want to get drunk' in the Manic Street Preachers' 'A Design for Life'.

But then it's interesting how few unequivocal hooray-for-booze songs there are. Addiction, depression and premature death keep creeping in, especially in country music, which is stuffed to the rafters with maudlin cowpokes drinking to forget the women that done them wrong. As you'd expect, many of those who have written most articulately about booze – Elliott Smith, Mark Eitzel, Jeff Tweedy – drank too much of it.

As did Paul Westerberg of the Replacements. In the mid-1980s the Minneapolis band blew their chances of a commercial breakthrough by getting blazing drunk and swearing on *Saturday Night Live*. The 97-second 'Beer for Breakfast' finds them at their liveliest.

In 'Streams of Whiskey', Shane MacGowan dreams that Brendan Behan advises him that the answers to all of life's problems do indeed lie at the bottom of a glass. We move from whiskey to brandy with the Streets' rowdy, lurching chronicle of an all-night bender in Amsterdam. Nouvelle Vague's bossa nova reinventions of punk classics are hit and miss, but here they deftly relocate the Dead Kennedys' delinquent anthem to a Parisian cocktail party. Full marks to singer Camille for sounding genuinely half-cut.

Back when their West Coast peers were painting themselves as brutal, unyielding killing machines (*plus ça change*), Tha Alkaholiks were a bunch of party-hearty stumblebums rapping about throwing up and wooing, er, physically unappealing women. Their signature tune is so good-natured that it includes a warning against drink driving. Two angles on alcoholism next: a young Nina Simone covers a Prohibition-era blues standard and Gil Scott-Heron, whose Achilles heel turned out to be not drink but crack cocaine, casts a sympathetic eye over alcohol's poorest victims.

During the 1970s, Tom Waits specialised in Hopperesque vignettes of LA nighthawks. Delivered in a woozy slur, 'The Piano Has Been Drinking (Not Me)' should ideally be played in a dimly lit dive, amid a blue haze of cigarette smoke, just before closing time. Then it's the mother of all morning-after country songs, Kris Kristofferson's 'Sunday Morning Coming Down'. Boasting a cinematic grandeur that Johnny Cash's version couldn't touch, it gave radio programmers palpitations with its line about having a beer for breakfast and 'another for dessert'.

Time to sober up. Having weaned himself off drugs but onto alcohol, in 1981 Lou Reed joined Alcoholics Anonymous, holed up in rural New Jersey and wrote 'The Last Shot' about his struggle to go straight. The shot of the title is both his last drink and his last chance.

THE PLAYLIST

Beer for Breakfast The Replacements

Streams of Whiskey The Pogues

Too Much Brandy The Streets

Too Drunk to Fuck Nouvelle Vague

Only When I'm Drunk Tha Alkaholiks

Gin House Blues Nina Simone

The Bottle Gil Scott-Heron and Brian Jackson

The Piano Has Been Drinking (Not Me) Tom Waits

Sunday Morning Coming Down Kris Kristofferson

The Last Shot Lou Reed

CHRISTMAS
SONGS

(▶) One Christmas, many years ago, I worked in Woolworths. After hearing 'Wonderful Christmas Time' for the ninety-third time on the endlessly repeated CD of festive hits I wanted to kill Paul McCartney – literally kill him – and I *like* Paul McCartney. Imagine what I wanted to do to Cliff Richard. Sometimes it feels like we're doomed to have the same Yuletide soundtrack for the rest of our lives, as if the 1970s never ended. Scientists predict that, unless we discover new sources, reserves of Slade and Wizzard will be exhausted by 2040.

The festive flame is being kept alive mainly by American indie bands who will knock off a lo-fi version of 'Little Drummer Boy' at the drop of a semi-ironic trucker's cap. But be careful what you play over lunch. 'Tis not just the season to be jolly; 'tis also the season to sing about drug addiction (Aimee Mann), alcoholism (The Handsome Family) and child abuse (De La Soul).

Phil Spector's *A Christmas Gift for You* remains the benchmark Christmas album. Tempting though it is to start with Spector's own spoken-word track, convincingly delivered in the style of a paedophile, Darlene Love's gargantuan melodrama is less likely to make children cry and adults shudder. 'I Was Born on Christmas Day', by Spector enthusiasts Saint Etienne, is wistful disco-pop that sparkles like tinsel.

The Ramones were running on fumes by 1989 but still triumphed with this romping plea for Yuletide détente. An unlikely Christmas album emerged from dauntingly cutting-edge New York New Wave label Ze in 1981. The fizzing, funky highlight was 'Christmas Wrapping' by the Waitresses: dance-around-the-Christmas-tree music for Brooklyn hipsters.

Political protest rarely intrudes on Christmas songs. On *Soulful Christmas*, one of his three festive albums, James Brown instructs Santa Claus to go where he's most needed. 'Tell 'em James Brown sent you,' he barks, perhaps fearing for the safety of a portly, affluent white man venturing into the heart of the Bronx in 1968. Sounds like Santa would also be welcome in Minneapolis, judging by Tom Waits's deliciously sad Christmas card from a prostitute trying and failing to make it a happy new year.

From the aforementioned American indie camp comes husband-and-wife duo Joy Zipper, with their sublime, acid-dipped sunshine pop: 'I love you more than a thousand Christmases.' Low, a trio of Minnesota Mormons, took a holiday from their usual funereal ambience in 1999 to make the best Christmas album of recent years. The sleighbell-shaking winter travelogue 'Just Like Christmas' could make even the Grinch smile.

Two customised standards to round off the list. First Otis Redding's epic, idiosyncratic reading of 'White Christmas', whose impassioned finale – 'May your days, May your DAYS, be merry, be *me-e-rry*, so *ME-E-RRY*' – makes every other version sound smug and shallow. And if you really need an antidote to 'Wonderful Christmas Time's saccharine good cheer, then Simon and Garfunkel's use of 'Silent Night' as the backdrop to a 1966 news broadcast stuffed with unrest, war and murder should do the trick.

THE PLAYLIST

Christmas (Baby Please Come Home) Darlene Love
I Was Born on Christmas Day Saint Etienne
Merry Christmas (I Don't Want to Fight Tonight)
   The Ramones
Christmas Wrapping The Waitresses
Santa Claus Go Straight to the Ghetto James Brown
Christmas Card from a Hooker in Minneapolis Tom Waits
Christmas Song Joy Zipper
Just Like Christmas Low
White Christmas Otis Redding
7 O'Clock News / Silent Night Simon and Garfunkel

COVER VERSIONS
BETTER THAN THE ORIGINAL SONGS

(▶) A cover version holds up a mirror to a band's soul, because the best musicians are invariably the best listeners. Those with imagination and guts can make a song their own while respecting its essence. Those with neither will either maul a favourite song to death or kill it with kindness, embalming it in timid reverence. For example, Razorlight's cretinous version of OutKast's 'Hey Ya!' tells you all you need to know about the band: namely that you should never listen to anything they do ever again.

One surefire way to reinvent a song is to flip the sex of the singer. Patti Smith introduced bisexuality and religious guilt (or rather its absence) to Them's horny garage-rocker 'Gloria', while Tricky granted the lead vocal of Public Enemy's 'Black Steel in the Hour of Chaos' to middle-class English girl Martina Topley-Bird. Wrenching the lyrics about an incarcerated Vietnam draft-dodger ('a brother like me', 'I'm a black man') completely out of context and replacing militant funk with scalding guitars, 'Black Steel' is a masterpiece of dislocation. With similar daring, Saint Etienne reincarnated Neil Young's creaky country-rock waltz as dreamy Balearic dub.

It's much harder to flesh a song out than to strip it down. Philadelphia soul singer Billy Paul whipped Elton John's ponderous 'Your Song' into a sustained six-minute burst of unadulterated joy, while Isaac Hayes approached Jimmy Webb's 'By the Time I Get to Phoenix' like he was adapting a short story into an epic screenplay. Speaking in his full-cream baritone, he reimagines the song's entire context so persuasively that by the time he starts singing, around the nine-minute mark, the emotional force knocks you off your feet. John Coltrane, another genius at arrangement, had the wit and imagination to transform *The Sound of Music*'s perky pick-me-up 'My Favourite Things' into a ceaselessly engaging jazz landmark.

An exceptional cover version is a form of theft. Hendrix stole 'All Along the Watchtower' from Dylan and never gave it back; Aretha Franklin hijacked Otis Redding's 'Respect' for ever. By turning Tim Buckley's 'Song to the Siren' into a tremulous ambient hymn, This Mortal Coil and Elizabeth Fraser made the original version seem like a mere sketch. A decade on, Buckley's son Jeff redressed the balance. A classic song hamstrung by chintzy 1980s production, Leonard Cohen's 'Hallelujah' was reborn as a modern standard by John Cale in 1991 and completely redefined by Buckley's matter-of-life-and-death intensity.

During his winter years, the Bible-black authority of Cash's voice produced several alchemical covers but none more transcendent than 'Hurt'. Winnowing the callow self-pity from Nine Inch Nails' junkie confessional ('crown of shit' wisely becomes 'crown of thorns'), he turned it into an old man's devastating deathbed testimonial. Finally, the Knife's shivery electro-pop was remade as a lump-in-the-throat ballad by fellow Swede José González and popularised by an advert for fancy TVs. Let's give fervent thanks that Razorlight didn't get to it first.

THE PLAYLIST

Gloria Patti Smith
Black Steel Tricky
Only Love Can Break Your Heart Saint Etienne
Your Song Billy Paul
By the Time I Get to Phoenix Isaac Hayes
My Favourite Things John Coltrane
Song to the Siren This Mortal Coil
Hallelujah Jeff Buckley
Hurt Johnny Cash
Heartbeats José González

SONGS ABOUT
SPACE TRAVEL

▶ Thoughts of the cosmos inspire erratic behaviour. Take, for example, the musical career of *Star Trek*'s Leonard Nimoy or the regrettable title of Thievery Corporation's *2001: A Spliff Odyssey*. Used wisely, however, lyrics about space travel can convey several different messages: you are an alienated rock star (Radiohead's 'Subterranean Homesick Alien'), you worry about the environment (Neil Young's 'After the Gold Rush'), you are a great fan of LSD (Hawkwind's 'Master of the Universe'), you are desperately short of ideas ('Solar System' by the Beach Boys), and so on.

Trailblazing 1960s producer Joe Meek was obsessed by space travel and his biggest hit, 'Telstar', still sounds full of unearthly promise. It evokes a bygone era of starry-eyed Dan Dare optimism, its sound effects whizzing by like rockets. Soon enough, though, the idea of being alone among the stars inspired a rich vein of melancholy, running through David Bowie's 'Space Oddity', Elton John's 'Rocket Man' and this disorientating acid-blues adventure from the Rolling Stones' short-lived psychedelic-wizard phase.

Bringing B-movie aesthetics to new wave, the B-52's meet a woman from Planet Claire, where 'all the trees are red / No one ever dies there / No one has a head.' Mixing the suspenseful riff from

Henry Mancini's *Peter Gunn* theme with suitably *Star Trek*-like keyboard sounds, it could be the title tune to the world's strangest sci-fi show. Don't let Sarah Brightman's 'I Lost My Heart to a Starship Trooper' put you off intergalactic romance. French singer Sheila and B Devotion hooked up with a 'star chaser' on the soaring 'Spacer', produced by disco mavens Chic.

I'm not sure what Captain Beefheart's 'Big Eyed Beans from Venus' really means, just as I'm not sure what most Captain Beefheart songs really mean, but the intrigue only enhances its thrilling extraterrestrial blues. On 'Third Stone from the Sun's dreamy, oscillating space-rock, Jimi Hendrix assumes the role of an alien visitor who likes Earth's chickens but not its humans and warns: 'You'll never hear surf music again.' Dick Dale must have been worried.

In the interests of research, I attempted to complete Sun Ra's free-jazz marathon 'Space Is the Place' but broke down midway through and turned to the Jonzun Crew's similarly titled electro gem, which fuses Kraftwerk's gleaming circuitry to George Clinton's cosmically inclined P-Funk. Kraftwerk's own 'Spacelab' was futuristic even by their bold standards – this airy, pulsing instrumental sounds like the missing link between the BBC Radiophonic Workshop and acid house.

In the 1970s Canadian music teacher Hans Fenger recorded his pupils singing pop hits with booming, rudimentary arrangements. The recordings, since reissued on CD, became cult artefacts and the highlight is this bizarre cover of David Bowie's 'Space Oddity', which propels the song into some vast and eerie new orbit. Finally, the Only Ones snap us back into life with a fizzing ode to girls, planets and, er, heroin. Lots and lots of heroin.

THE PLAYLIST

Telstar The Tornados

2000 Light Years from Home The Rolling Stones

Planet Claire The B-52's

Spacer Sheila and the B Devotion

Big Eyed Beans from Venus Captain Beefheart

Third Stone from the Sun The Jimi Hendrix Experience

Space Is the Place The Jonzun Crew

Spacelab Kraftwerk

Space Oddity The Langley Schools Music Project

Another Girl, Another Planet The Only Ones

FAMOUS PEOPLE

(▶) Pop music can be enormously educational. Were it not for Boney M, nobody would have realised that Rasputin was Russia's greatest love machine, and without Black Grape the fact that Neil Armstrong has balls bigger than King Kong would have remained an Armstrong family secret.

Songs about famous names also tell us about the songwriters. Steve Earle proved his mettle by exploring the motivations of John Walker Lindh, the so-called 'American Taliban', while The Cult's 'Edie (Ciao Baby)', their banal tribute to Warhol model Edie Sedgwick, usefully confirmed that they were posturing buffoons. The Magnetic Fields' 'The Death of Ferdinand de Saussure' tells us that Stephin Merritt likes to make semioticians titter knowingly.

Lazy songwriters head straight for the icons – James Dean, Marilyn Monroe, Muhammad Ali – but Half Man Half Biscuit's Nigel Blackwell prefers to immortalise post-war cricketers ('Fuckin' 'Ell It's Fred Titmus') and snooker referees ('The Len Ganley Stance'). On this 2001 single he puzzles over the televisual appeal of former Arsenal goalkeeper Bob Wilson. Next up, Modern Lovers' envious proto-punk dissertation on the womanising skills of Pablo Picasso.

Musicians' enduring fascination with murderers can cause problems – German cannibal Armin Meiwes sued Rammstein for basing a song on his case – so it's safer to write about the deceased. The Adverts were intrigued by murderer Gary Gilmore's unorthodox death row request to donate his eyes for transplant, and indie darling Sufjan Stevens distilled the life of 'killer clown' John Wayne Gacy, Jr into an eerie aural biography. Chirpy ska star Prince Buster was less concerned with psychological motivation than with spelling: 'C-A-P-O-N-E. Capone!' I told you pop was educational.

List songs often seem like crass attempts to share a platform with past greats but Stevie Wonder's 'Black Man' is different because it shines a light on forgotten pioneers. Wonder marked America's bicentennial with a plea for racial harmony wrapped in a call-and-response history lesson and bundled in joyous funk.

Similarly, the Manic Street Preachers made millions aware of Kevin Carter, the troubled photojournalist who committed suicide in 1994, shortly after winning a Pulitzer for his work in Sudan. It's one of their best singles too, all stabbing punk-funk and rat-a-tat vocals. 'All for You, Sophia', the fantastic B-side to 'Take Me Out', is a double word score: a song from one Franz Ferdinand to another. Sophia was the Austrian archduke's wife, killed by the same assassin. Unfortunately for GCSE history students, the band never explored the other causes of the First World War; perhaps the Kaiser Chiefs can be persuaded to write about the dispute over Alsace-Lorraine.

Movie stars tend to prompt daydreams. Bananarama contrasted their own drab romantic encounters with the bilingual charms of Robert De Niro (it would have been Al Pacino but his name didn't scan as well) and Woody Guthrie, covered here by Billy Bragg and Wilco, invited Ingrid Bergman to join him on the Italian island of Stromboli. I'm not sure she went but you can't blame him for asking.

THE PLAYLIST

Bob Wilson – Anchorman Half Man Half Biscuit
Pablo Picasso The Modern Lovers
Gary Gilmore's Eyes The Adverts
John Wayne Gacy, Jr Sufjan Stevens
Al Capone Prince Buster
Black Man Stevie Wonder
Kevin Carter Manic Street Preachers
All for You, Sophia Franz Ferdinand
Robert De Niro's Waiting Bananarama
Ingrid Bergman Billy Bragg and Wilco

SONGS ABOUT
FIRE

▶ In November 1966, a frazzled Brian Wilson was toiling over his magnum opus, *Smile*, little realising that it would take thirty-eight years to complete. For the section entitled 'Fire' he insisted the string section wear fire helmets, and asked the janitor to start a small blaze in a bucket so that the musicians could smell smoke as they played. Later that night, Wilson heard that a nearby warehouse had burned down, decided (naturally) that he had caused the conflagration and locked away the tapes in horror.

Trust Wilson to find fire terrifying rather than exciting. For most songwriters, flames represent love, dancing, rage: passion of every variety. They are rarely intended literally. In real life, the title of the Trammps' 'Disco Inferno' would be a distressing newspaper headline, and Busta Rhymes's 'Light Your Ass On Fire' would constitute catastrophically bad advice.

Obvious it may be, but there is no better way to open a playlist than Arthur Brown hollering, 'I am the lord of hellfire! And I bring you . . .' Far more genuinely sinister is one of the songs that launched Brian Eno's post-Roxy Music solo career. The mystery and menace of 'Baby's On Fire' owes as much to Robert Fripp's infernal guitar solo as it does to Eno's vocal villainy.

More than any other record, Jerry Lee Lewis's giant roar of lust explains why early rock 'n' roll ignited such outrage. You can picture the aghast reactions of 1950s parents: '*This* is what our kids are listening to?!?' Two subsequent moral panics – punk and rave – were smashed together on the Prodigy's thrillingly antisocial 'Firestarter'. Enraging parents when the video was shown on *Top of the Pops*, it still sounds like a riot in progress: a kickdrum like a punch to the gut, an electronic squeal like tyres on tarmac and Keith Flint's malevolent Essex-demon jabber.

The next sounds you'll hear are an alarm bell and a fire engine's siren. In reggae and punk, fire has a righteous, cleansing quality, scorching away perceived sins. Recorded as riots swept Britain in 1979, and the best song The Clash never recorded, the Ruts' unbearably tense 'Babylon's Burning' gleefully anticipates the fiery demise of western civilisation. A decade later, Public Enemy delivered an incendiary rant against Hollywood's portrayal of black people: 'butlers and maids, slaves and hos'. Steve Albini's Big Black, meanwhile, recommended torching smalltown America simply to alleviate the boredom of living there. 'Kerosene's metallic groove rumbles and clanks for three minutes before erupting into a glorious pyromaniac's manifesto.

Had you been on a New York dancefloor in 1983, you might have heard the next two tunes back to back. Talking Heads' wonderfuly eerie floor-filler was inspired by the crowd at a Funkadelic concert shouting 'burn down the house', but Byrne's anxious, stabbing delivery implies that he's taking it literally. Across town, Madonna was emerging as the scenester-most-likely-to, and 'Burning Up' combines erotic heat with disco fever. Super Furry Animals play us out with 'Fire in My Heart', which sounds like a children's hymn recorded on a space station by Brian Wilson. Fire helmet optional.

THE PLAYLIST

Fire The Crazy World of Arthur Brown

Baby's On Fire Brian Eno

Great Balls of Fire Jerry Lee Lewis

Firestarter The Prodigy

Babylon's Burning The Ruts

Burn Hollywood Burn Public Enemy

Kerosene Big Black

Burning Down the House Talking Heads

Burning Up Madonna

Fire in My Heart Super Furry Animals

JOYOUS
SONGS

(▶) My favourite scene in the documentary *Touching the Void* finds
hapless mountaineer Joe Simpson at death's door. Crazed by pain,
malnutrition and hypothermia, Simpson's brain decides to torture him
with an endless loop of Boney M's 'Brown Girl in the Ring'. If I'm ever
pinned to the floor for several days by an avalanche of badly stacked
CDs, I expect the music whirring demonically around my head to be
'Walking on Sunshine' by Katrina and the Waves.

There are other allegedly happy songs that drive me insane,
including the B-52's 'Love Shack' and REM's egregious 'Shiny Happy
People'. Every reader must have their own cheery *bête noire*, which
has found them leaving a wedding dancefloor in disgust while fellow
guests stampeded in the opposite direction. These ten songs lift my
spirits. I can't guarantee everyone will agree.

Ian Dury's 'Reasons to Be Cheerful (Part 3)' is virtually a self-help
book, itemising some of the things that make life worth living:
'Cheddar cheese and pickle, the Vincent motorcycle.' The Go! Team's
irresistible 'Bottle Rocket' can turn any dancefloor into a playground,
its primary-coloured samples bumping into each other like tartrazine-
fevered toddlers. 'It's Alright, I Feel It' is Nuyorican Soul's disco-

homaging celebration of music itself.

Youth informs the next two songs. Capturing the simple joys of late adolescence as well as anyone since surf-era Beach Boys, Supergrass's 'Alright' locates galaxies of pleasure in a cigarette, a first pay-packet, a fast car, a one-night stand. Sinatra's 'You Make Me Feel So Young', meanwhile, is especially treasurable for the image of the Mafia-connected 'chairman of the board' picking forget-me-nots. Like a girl.

Another Frank, another love song. Soul music has added immeasurably to the sum of human happiness but you don't need telling about Stevie Wonder and Marvin Gaye, so here's a less well-known gem from Motown in-house songwriter Frank Wilson. His heart-pounding testament to the euphoria of love was once the rarest northern soul record, with one of only two extant copies selling for £15,000; now you can download it for 79p. Honestly, we don't know we're born. Neil Diamond was also a hired hand (for the Brill Building hit factory) when he wrote the explosively happy 'I'm a Believer' for the Monkees: a marriage made in pop heaven.

Happy songs are more complex when they reflect on life's bleaker aspects. Just as Ice Cube's 'It Was a Good Day' revelled in a rare respite from ducking bullets, 'Mr E's Beautiful Blues' ponders people's ability to be cheerful despite the crap that surrounds them. If you're in a good mood, don't listen too closely to the verses.

Another classic from the soul crates, Marlena Shaw's reading of

'California Soul' is the closest you can get to aural Prozac. Love, music, sunshine: it's all here. After so much jollity, the Zombies' impossibly tender 'This Will Be Our Year' closes the playlist on a thoughtful note, its two beleaguered lovers bruised yet optimistic, convinced that better days will come.

THE PLAYLIST

Reasons to Be Cheerful (Part 3) Ian Dury and the Blockheads
Bottle Rocket The Go! Team
It's Alright, I Feel It Nuyorican Soul
Alright Supergrass
You Make Me Feel So Young Frank Sinatra
Do I Love You (Indeed I Do) Frank Wilson
I'm a Believer The Monkees
Mr E's Beautiful Blues Eels
California Soul Marlena Shaw
This Will Be Our Year The Zombies

SONGS ABOUT
CHILDREN

(▶) In his song 'I Don't Wanna Grow Up', Tom Waits's prepubescent narrator asks, in a suspiciously postpubescent growl, 'How do you move in a world of fog that's always changing things?' In 'The End of the Rainbow', Richard Thompson informs his presumably distraught son, 'There's nothing to grow up for any more.' Even Stevie Wonder, a glass-half-full kind of guy, sighs in 'I Wish', 'I wish those days could come back once more.'

Again and again, you get skewed visions of childhood bliss and adult misery from grown-up Christopher Robins who quietly mourn the day they sent Winnie the Pooh packing. Personally, I reckon nostalgia's got too much in common with indie snobbery: it makes you overrate the early material. 'Yeah, my life's OK now but you should have seen me before I got big and sold out.'

From anyone other than Moby Grape casualty Skip Spence, 'Little Hands's children-of-the-world lyrics would be poisonously sweet, but acid-damaged naifs never quite grasp how creepy and fractured their attempted innocence sounds, and how much it is coloured by adult sadness.

The power ballad was invented to allow rock pigs to pretend that beneath that hell-raising, groupie-ravishing exterior hides a fragile soul who just wants to be wuvved – this, of course, being a good way to expedite further groupie-ravishing. 'Sweet Child o' Mine's ode to a lover who brings back memories of 'a warm safe place' excels because the vulnerability rings true. Also, that riff is just ridiculous.

All happy childhoods resemble one another; each unhappy childhood is unhappy in its own way. Black Box Recorder recount a very English kind of passive resistance with the singsong punchline, 'Life is unfair / Kill yourself or get over it,' but Ghostface Killah seems weirdly nostalgic for his belt-wielding mother's tough love: 'Despite the alcohol, I had a great old mama.'

There's an eerie magic to 'Neighbourhood #1 (Tunnels)', Arcade Fire's tale of adventure and loss in a snowbound, parentless world. It's terrain that Björk might enjoy, judging by the Svankmajeresque wonderland of spiders, ravens and cigar-smoking five-year-olds she describes in the Sugarcubes' slippery, dreamlike 'Birthday'.

There's no joy to be derived from parental absence in the Carter Family's impossibly bleak 'Poor Orphan Child', lashed by the harsh winds of the Depression. The Carter Family call on God for help, but an aching Donny Hathaway tells the benighted subject of 'Little Ghetto Boy' that he has to break the cycle of gloom himself: 'You've gotta fight to make it better.'

It's not often I'm moved by the Gallagher brothers, but 'Fade Away' replaces their usual can-do triumphalism with fierce longing. Written before they made it big, it vibrates with doubt: 'While we're living / The dreams we have as children fade away.' Finally, acid-folk ingenue Devendra Banhart insists on remaining a child, 'from being my daddy's sperm to being packed in an urn', while hinting that such behaviour, though fun for him, would be unbelievably irritating for everyone else.

THE PLAYLIST

Little Hands Skip Spence
Sweet Child o' Mine Guns 'n' Roses
Child Psychology Black Box Recorder
Whip You with a Strap Ghostface Killah
Neighbourhood #1 (Tunnels) Arcade Fire
Birthday Sugarcubes
Poor Orphan Child The Carter Family
Little Ghetto Boy Donny Hathaway
Fade Away Oasis
I Feel Just Like a Child Devendra Banhart

US CITIES AND STATES

▶ The USA is the only country in the world with a map you can hum. So many singers have brought out the music lurking in its place names: the racing syllables of Chuck Berry's San Bernardino, the wide-open vowels of Lynyrd Skynyrd's Alabama, the long, guilt-wracked final *a* in Gene Pitney's Tulsa.

I've covered New York and California elsewhere in this book, so the south provided the most possibilities, whether for good ('Georgia On My Mind') or ill (Neil Young's 'Alabama'). Residents of neglected states such as Wisconsin, Connecticut and South Dakota, hang on in there. How many outsiders had heard of Wichita before Jimmy Webb's lineman fetched up there?

Let's commence on a note of civic pride. Like many jazz standards, 'Do You Know What It Means to Miss New Orleans?' originated in a movie (1947's *New Orleans*), then found a life of its own. After Hurricane Katrina, it dripped with a deeper kind of longing, as much an elegy as a tribute. The Standells' garage-rock classic 'Dirty Water', written by the same man as 'Tainted Love', Ed Cobb, saluted Boston in all its grimy glory; even now that the Charles River has been cleaned up, it remains the Red Sox' victory anthem. Jackson, Mississippi is the venue for Johnny and June's comic bickering.

Most pop odysseys end amid the lights of New York or Los Angeles, but there's always the return journey to consider. Gladys Knight's lover packs up his dashed dreams and leaves LA for Georgia ('goin' back to find what's left of his world') on an aching soul cut originally titled 'Midnight Plane to Houston'. Michelle Shocked's 'Anchorage' tells of two Texan schoolfriends parting ways: one to find fame in New York, the other to raise a family in 'the biggest state in the union'.

Some locations attract jeers, not cheers. Courtney Love thumbs her nose at the cliquey riot grrrl scene of Olympia, Washington on this ragged, troublemaking Hole B-side, while Public Enemy head for Arizona, enraged by the governor's refusal to observe Martin Luther King Day. 'I'm on the one mission / To get a politician / To honour or he's a goner,' booms Chuck D on a gospel-funk juggernaut that moves like a military convoy.

Nina Simone damned an entire state in her rage over racist crimes including the 1963 assassination of civil rights activist Medgar Evers. On this debut live recording, listen to the way she first lulls the unwitting audience into laughter, then stuns it into silence with the scalding heat of her indignation.

Finally, two deft portraits of cities. Country outsiders the Flatlanders survey Dallas from an aeroplane window and see a jewel, a jungle, a ruthless woman, 'a rich man with a death wish in his eyes'. Long before *The Wire*, Randy Newman held up poor old Baltimore as the acme of urban despair on this devastating lament. If I ever go to Baltimore (I must say he doesn't make it sound tempting), then I won't be able to stop singing it.

THE PLAYLIST

Do You Know What It Means to Miss New Orleans?
   Louis Armstrong

Dirty Water The Standells

Jackson Johnny Cash and June Carter

Midnight Train to Georgia Gladys Knight and the Pips

Anchorage Michelle Shocked

Olympia Hole

By the Time I Get to Arizona Public Enemy

Mississippi Goddam Nina Simone

Dallas The Flatlanders

Baltimore Randy Newman

PHONE CALLS AND LETTERS

(▶) Before we start, let's forgive the telephone for blotting the copybook of soul's greatest genius by inspiring Stevie Wonder, in a moment of weakness, to compose 'I Just Called to Say I Love You', and move on to songs which exploit ideas of distance and longing without making the listener feel queasy. Letters are equally evocative but email has yet to produce a single great song. Perhaps it's because letters are intrinsically dramatic – there is no telling when, or even if, they will reach their destination – whereas emails are blandly immediate unless you have server problems. Nobody wants to sing about server problems.

'Hanging on the Telephone' opens the playlist with the sound of a ringing phone and two and a half minutes of punk-pop perfection. On 'Hello Operator', proud mobile phone refusenik Jack White opts to use an operator like in days of yore. As if even this were too new-fangled, by the second verse he's trying to get his message delivered via canary.

Post-punk oddities Department S scored their sole hit in 1981 with the deliciously puzzling 'Is Vic There?', twisting the mystery caller's prosaic query into the voice of creeping insanity. Paranoia also vibrates through 'Telephone Thing'. For reasons known only to Mark

E. Smith, the Fall's neurotically funky, Coldcut-produced rant against surveillance snoops singles out the actress who played Ethel in *EastEnders*: 'You Gretchen Franklin nosy matron type.'

Text messages make a rare appearance on MIA's 'URAQT', a stroppy retort to a love rival ('You fucking with my man and you text him all the time') which bounces along like a skipping-rope chant. Telegrams get their due on 'Hey, Western Union Man', Jerry Butler's impassioned attempt to contact an aggrieved girlfriend who won't answer his phone calls. He's out of luck now; Western Union finally shut down its telegraph service in January 2006.

Most letter songs feature absent lovers, and none convey the breathless excitement of receiving a long-awaited missive better than the Box Tops' blue-eyed soul classic 'The Letter'. Hard to believe that gruff lead singer Alex Chilton, who later formed Big Star, was only sixteen at the time. Sarah Vaughan, performing lonesome jazz standard 'I'm Gonna Sit Right Down and Write Myself a Letter', is reduced to penning her own love letters, complete with kisses at the bottom.

Songs such as the Zombies' 'Care Of Cell 44' are written in the form of letters. In Linton Kwesi Johnson's 'Sonny's Lettah', a Jamaican immigrant who runs afoul of Britain's notorious sus laws writes to his mother to explain how he ended up in jail. In its awkward, apologetic formality ('I don't know how to tell you this'), it's heartbreakingly credible.

The best epistolary song of all, though, is Eminem's 'Stan', a masterpiece of escalating desparation that exploits the conceit to its fullest; you can even hear pencil skidding across paper. With chilling elegance, it recognises that a letter is a one-sided conversation, written in the hope of a reply that may never come. Please Mr Postman indeed.

THE PLAYLIST

Hanging on the Telephone Blondie
Hello Operator The White Stripes
Is Vic There? Department S
Telephone Thing The Fall
URAQT MIA
Hey, Western Union Man Jerry Butler
The Letter The Box Tops
I'm Gonna Sit Right Down and Write Myself a Letter
  Sarah Vaughan
Sonny's Lettah (Anti Sus Poem) Linton Kwesi Johnson
Stan Eminem

SONGS ABOUT
WAR

(▶) War, as Bill Withers sighed, is 'one big drag'. The challenge for songwriters is to animate this obvious truism with fresh insight – unlike Boy George, who will never live down his deathless observation that 'War is stupid and people are stupid.' Honorary mentions to rock's keenest military historians: Al Stewart gives Anthony Beevor a run for his money on the insanely detailed 'Roads to Moscow' and Iron Maiden have ranged from Alexander the Great's conquest of Persia to the Battle of Britain. I'm not saying the songs are good, mind.

Edwin Starr died two weeks after the invasion of Iraq, and his signature tune, played as a tribute, still had work to do. Between Starr's drill-sergeant holler and producer Norman Whitfield's surgical-strike brass stabs, it's a marvellous contradiction: bellicose pacifism. Surely the reason Vietnam inspired so many songs is because conscription gave the conflict such ghastly immediacy. In summer 1969, Country Joe and the Fish roused crowds at Woodstock with their bitterly jaunty jugband singalong. That December, the conflict's first draft lottery took place. You can't help wondering if some of the festival-goers chanting 'Whoopee, we're all gonna die!' on the live album ended up doing just that.

Eric B and Rakim's 1992 track still resonates with its account of a Muslim GI in the first Gulf War. The final verse is freakishly prescient: 'Remember Pearl Harbor? / New York could be over, G / Kamikaze strapped with bombs.' In '30 Seconds over Tokyo', Pere Ubu's David Thomas imagines himself a bomber pilot while his bandmates simulate the engines' ominous drone. Recorded in 1975, this claustrophobic art-rock was post-punk before there was any punk to be post.

In 1938, Norbert Schultze set to music a First World War poem about a lone sentry and saw 'Lili Marleen' become massively popular among armies on both sides in the Second. I've chosen the German version by anti-Nazi expat Marlene Dietrich. The Manic Street Preachers' elegiac Spanish Civil War song, inspired by George Orwell and the Clash, raises chewy questions about the notion of justified intervention and the distinction between pacifism and appeasement.

The economics of war often inspire trite blood-for-oil clichés or caricatures of cackling arms dealers. One deft exception is 'Shipbuilding', which ponders the Falklands War's impact on a dockworking community. Elvis Costello wrote the song; Robert Wyatt's bottomlessly sad delivery made it a masterpiece. Remaining on the home front, Kate Bush portrays a grieving mother on the eerily lush 'Army Dreamers'.

Bill Withers unites two traditions of war song – the letter home (see Tom Waits's 'Day After Tomorrow') and the maimed soldier's lament (Metallica's 'One') – on his wise and moving story about a soldier who loses his right arm in Vietnam. Another disfigured conscript narrates 'And the Band Played Waltzing Matilda', in which songwriter Eric Bogle uses the massacre of ANZAC forces at Gallipoli to comment on Vietnam. Undeterred by not being Australian, the Pogues performed the definitive rendition. The combatants may have changed but the sentiment is ageless.

THE PLAYLIST

War Edwin Starr

I-Feel-Like-I'm-Fixin'-to-Die Rag Country Joe and the Fish

Casualties of War Eric B and Rakim

30 Seconds over Tokyo Pere Ubu

Lili Marleen Marlene Dietrich

If You Tolerate This Then Your Children Will Be Next
   Manic Street Preachers

Shipbuilding Robert Wyatt

Army Dreamers Kate Bush

I Can't Write Left-Handed Bill Withers

And the Band Played Waltzing Matilda The Pogues

UPBEAT BREAK-UP
SONGS

(▶) So what exactly qualifies as an upbeat break-up song? To help me decide this playlist, I applied the Bonnie 'Prince' Billy test. Many gloomy lyrics are cloaked in party-hearty melodies so I simply imagined each song performed by the fuzz-faced alt-country miseryguts. *Voilà!* The Jackson 5's 'I Want You Back' is revealed as a wail of impotent desperation. I thus discounted anything petty, whiny, mopey, needy, vengeful or irate. A degree of I-don't-need-you bitchiness snuck in but only when it sounded truly victorious.

The prime example is McAlmont and Butler's 'Yes'. This fondly remembered Britpop one-off is a spectacular piece of work, big and brash enough to be a Motown classic; McAlmont transmutes his wounded pride into a rush of joy and triumph. Belle and Sebastian's 'I'm Waking Up to Us' is their Fleetwood Mac moment, an eye-wateringly frank account of the collapsing love affair between frontman Stuart Murdoch and cellist Isobel Campbell. What makes it exceptional is the way Murdoch progresses from rancour to forgiveness. In the closing lines he declares: 'My anger turns to pity and to love.'

Gloria Gaynor's 'I Will Survive' is merely the tip of a big girly iceberg. If I included every example of women gutsily promising to soldier on, the playlist would resemble the soundtrack to *Bridget Jones's Diary*, so I've chosen just one. Whitney Houston's melismatic ballads bring me out in hives but she's all icy control on 'It's Not Right But It's OK', her phlegmatic farewell to a lousy cheat: 'I'd rather be alone than unhappy.' Similar sentiments fuel Dean Parrish's euphoric 'I'm On My Way', the last record ever played at northern soul mecca Wigan Casino.

The Avalanches make breaking up sound magical by weaving a snatch of forgotten blue-eyed soul group the Main Attraction ('Since I left you I found a world so new') through a lush tapestry of samples. Let's stay jaunty with 'Here I Go', in which Syd Barrett relates, with unflappable insouciance, how he broke up with a girl who didn't like his songs and hooked up with her more appreciative sister the very same day. Smooth work, Syd.

The two ex-lovers in the Human League's wonderfully tender 'Louise' meet by chance a few years later and part with the possibility of rekindling their affair. Frank Sinatra, meanwhile, is at his breeziest on George and Ira Gershwin's ode to those little things that make a relationship glow in the memory: 'The way you hold your knife / The way we danced 'til three.'

Songs which wish an ex nothing but the best are rarer than unicorns. File these last two songs alongside 'Don't Forget About Me' by Dusty Springfield and 'Caroline Goodbye' by Colin Blunstone as the most good-natured farewells imaginable. Rarely a forgiving songwriter, Ray Davies is atypically tender on 'Days', refusing to let hard feelings sour his memories. Diana Ross's neglected classic 'Remember Me' is happier still. As the music surges skyward, she has only one request: 'Remember me as a good thing.' What more can anyone ask?

THE PLAYLIST

Yes McAlmont and Butler

I'm Waking Up to Us Belle and Sebastian

It's Not Right But It's OK Whitney Houston

I'm On My Way Dean Parrish

Since I Left You The Avalanches

Here I Go Syd Barrett

Louise The Human League

They Can't Take That Away from Me Frank Sinatra

Days The Kinks

Remember Me Diana Ross

TREES, GRASS AND FLOWERS

(▶) Pitted against such racy topics as cars and guns, trees and hedgerows can't help but seem like eccentrically low-key subjects for a song: a form of musical downsizing. Stevie Wonder pruned down his fanbase in one fell swoop with his confounding double album *Journey Through the Secret Life of Plants* and Pulp bowed out with their own green-fingered opus, the sorely undervalued *We Love Life*.

You get two plants for the price of one on the Ink Spots' haunting 1940 hit 'Whispering Grass (Don't Tell the Trees)'. Its person-ification of trees as treacherous blabbermouths was reversed on Pulp's 'The Trees', in which they are mute witnesses who 'never said that you were leaving'. Either way the message is clear: don't trust the trees, they're bastards.

One thing that inspired an unusual interest in all things herbacious was good old LSD. *Mojo*'s excellent psychedelic boxset, *Acid Drops, Spacedust and Flying Saucers*, is overgrown with acid-dazzled longhairs sipping mushroom tea in English country gardens. One electrifying example is 'I Can Hear the Grass Grow', a top five hit which must have made many teenage listeners want some of what the Move were having. Dr Octagon's 'Blue Flowers' is a rare and wonderful example of psychedelic hip-hop; whereas the Move saw rainbows in the evening, rapper Kool Keith perceives green rain and purple pastures. M83's 'Run Into Flowers', a blast of heat-haze synths and flickering strings, completes the tripped-out trio.

Back to reality with the jaunty country-pop of Lynn Anderson's 'Rose Garden'. If you fancy a more melancholic alliance of roses and country music, you could substitute Elvis Costello's version of 'Good Year for the Roses', but I'm trying to keep spirits high in preparation for XTC's charmingly bawdy rural idyll, 'Grass'. Just listen to the relish with which Colin Moulding sings 'We'll take a tum-bull, excuse for a fum-bull.'

Sunshine and grass conspire to more disturbing effect on 'The Hissing of Summer Lawns', my favourite Joni Mitchell song. The music's eerie, jazzy languor echoes Mitchell's lyrical portrait of a kept woman wandering her lavishly appointed prison, the lawn sprinklers outside as sinister as snakes. But when it comes to the dark side of nature, nothing beats *The Wicker Man*. From Paul Giovanni's soundtrack, 'Maypole' is a cycle-of-life pagan chant that's creepy enough to put you off the countryside altogether. The danger that lurks in forests inspired Paul Weller's finest post-Jam moment, 'Wild Wood'. Portishead's subtly dramatic remix takes it to a higher plane, with Adrian Utley's twang-of-doom guitar an ominous counterpoint to Weller's own strumming.

A few years ago, Minnie Riperton's 'Les Fleur' (French grammar wasn't her strong point) was practically unknown; now it's such an acknowledged classic that it's been plundered for a Baileys advert. Written and produced by maverick genius Charles Stepney, it ascends from a rippling bed of cello and guitar to quite the most hair-raising, heart-pounding crescendo in pop history. Fittingly for a song about the symbolism of flowers, it makes you feel that bit more alive.

THE PLAYLIST

Whispering Grass (Don't Tell the Trees) The Ink Spots
I Can Hear the Grass Grow The Move
Blue Flowers Dr Octagon
Run Into Flowers M83
Rose Garden Lynn Anderson
Grass XTC
The Hissing of Summer Lawns Joni Mitchell
Maypole Paul Giovanni
Wild Wood (The Sheared Wood Remix) Paul Weller
Les Fleur Minnie Riperton

SCHOOL

▶ School has all of rock's vital ingredients: tension between discipline and rebellion (homework assignment: watch Richard Linklater's *School of Rock*); intimate friendships; vicious enmities; sexual awakenings; and enough traumatic experiences to sow the seeds of a healthy persecution complex that, with careful tending, will last you the rest of your days.

Songwriters take a somewhat jaundiced view of the teaching profession: its members are at best objects of erotic fixation and at worst despotic sadists filling their pupils' heads with poisonous lies and flinging blackboard rubbers at the sensitive, poetry-writing soul from 4B. Sting, himself a former teacher, did nothing to help their cause by writing 'Don't Stand So Close to Me', which, with its reference to 'the old man in that book by Nabokov', is at once creepy, clumsy and pretentious. C minus. See me later.

The playlist starts with Chuck Berry funnelling the elation of hearing the final bell into base-element rock 'n' roll. The Beach Boys' 'All Dressed Up for School' is just as uplifting if you skip past the slightly clammy rhapsodising over schoolgirl outfits. When they whoop 'new to school threads really do it to me', they sound a little too much like the old man in that book by Nabokov.

Madness's 'Baggy Trousers' invented its own genre: the bittersweet knees-up. There have been more sophisticated lyrics about school but none so bluntly evocative as 'Lots of girls and lots of boys / Lots of smells and lots of noise.' Busted's 'What I Go to School For' is the disarmingly frank story of having a crush on a teacher.

So much for good memories. Nirvana kick off the bad ones with a primal roar. The lyrics comprise just 15 words, including an indignant yowl of 'No recess!', but they get the job done. Belle and Sebastian could compile an album of songs about classroom politics; the pick of the bunch is 'Expectations', whose misfit heroine wins the heart of every indie boy by 'making life-size models of the Velvet Underground from clay'.

In Britain, at least, 'The Headmaster Ritual' is the *ne plus ultra* of school songs. Johnny Marr set out to compose 'what Joni Mitchell would have done had she been a punk rocker', while Morrissey tore into the 'belligerent ghouls' who 'run Manchester schools'. Neil Tennant's own memories of northern tyrants informed one of the Pet Shop Boys' most underrated songs, which uses samples of the 1936 Moscow show trials to imply a comparison with Soviet Russia, with its own grim-faced staff, viciously enthusiastic prefects and endless cruel varieties of detention.

Rufus Wainwright tenderly imagines a wealthy woman remembering her schoolgirl infatuation with the titular art teacher: 'He asked us what our favorite work of art was / But never could I tell him it was him.' And finally, there's the effervescent 'Starfish and Coffee', in which colourful nonconformity inspires celebration rather than persecution. And it's got a school bell on it. More songs should have school bells on them.

THE PLAYLIST

School Days (Ring Ring Goes the Bell) Chuck Berry

All Dressed Up for School The Beach Boys

Baggy Trousers Madness

What I Go to School For Busted

School Nirvana

Expectations Belle and Sebastian

The Headmaster Ritual The Smiths

This Must Be the Place I Waited Years to Leave
     Pet Shop Boys

The Art Teacher Rufus Wainwright

Starfish and Coffee Prince

COVERS OF BEATLES
SONGS

(▶) The Beatles' legacy has a split personality. The recordings themselves are zealously guarded from the attentions of compilations, adverts and sampler-wielding DJs. The songs, however, can be freely interpreted by any old clown. Nobody else's songbook has inspired cover versions by both Labour MP Derek Enright (who performed 'Eleanor Rigby' in Latin) and famed wabbit-hunter Elmer Fudd ('The Fool on the Hill').

You can buy whole albums of them, including genre-specific round-ups (*Motown Meets the Beatles*), movie soundtracks (*I Am Sam*) and tribute discs (*Sgt. Pepper Knew My Father*). Some are chilling prospects: do I really need to hear Pinky and Perky squeak through 'All My Loving' or US jam-band Phish get to work on 'Ob-La-Di Ob-La-Da'? No, I don't think I do.

As with all cover versions, triumph and travesty are in the ear of the beholder. Personally, I think that Joe Cocker strained and hollered all the charm out of 'With a Little Help from My Friends' and that Johnny Cash's death's-door reading of 'In My Life' sounds uncomfortably mawkish. Conversely, I've always had a soft spot for Candy Flip's oft-reviled 'Strawberry Fields Forever' because of its guileless MDMA-flooded optimism.

Motown's love affair with the Beatles produced wildly varying results. The best is Stevie Wonder's effervescent 'We Can Work It Out', a song perfectly suited to his own muscular optimism. Siouxsie and the Banshees played against type on 'Dear Prudence', cajoling post-punk out to play in the psychedelic sunshine. The Breeders' 'Happiness Is a Warm Gun' scorches away the original's playful coda, leaving only tension and violent sexuality.

If you're going to tackle the shatteringly innovative 'Tomorrow Never Knows', you'd better rebuild it from the ground up. For an inspired homage rather than a straight cover try the Chemical Brothers' 'Setting Sun', but here Phil Manzanera and Brian Eno construct their own hypnotic groove from funk bass and fluttering synthesisers, topped off by Eno's deadpan vocals. More radical still, Roots Manuva submerges every child's favourite Beatles song (and every adult's least favourite) beneath five fathoms of bad-trip dub.

Both these songs put a sinister spin on the Beatles' benign acid fantasias but neither flirts with madness quite like William Shatner's 'Lucy in the Sky with Diamonds'. The erstwhile Captain Kirk hurls himself into every line with lunatic zeal, like an undercover policeman pretending to take LSD in order to infiltrate a hippie drug ring. Like moonlighting actors, lounge artists were suckers for the Beatles; in the hands of Sergio Mendes and Brasil '66, 'The Fool on the Hill' becomes sun-kissed easy listening.

Time for some straighter readings. Emmylou Harris speaks to the tenderness and hush of 'Here, There and Everywhere', while Fiona Apple's sublime 'Across the Universe', recorded for the film *Pleasantville*, plays up the grandeur of the melody. She even has the same surname as the Beatles' record label. Tradition dictates that all Beatles compilations end with 'Hey Jude', so here's Wilson Pickett to sing us out with lung-busting gusto. All together now: 'Naa naa naa na-na na naaa . . .'

THE PLAYLIST

We Can Work It Out Stevie Wonder

Dear Prudence Siouxsie and the Banshees

Happiness Is a Warm Gun The Breeders

Tomorrow Never Knows 801

Yellow Submarine Roots Manuva

Lucy in the Sky with Diamonds William Shatner

The Fool on the Hill Sergio Mendes and Brasil '66

Here, There and Everywhere Emmylou Harris

Across the Universe Fiona Apple

Hey Jude Wilson Pickett

SONGS ABOUT
HOME

▶ Musicians have a vexed relationship with home. At best boring, at worst suffocating, it's something that needs to be left behind before you can get on with the business of living. Give a band a few months of hotels, tour buses and airport lounges, however, and cue the misty-eyed nostalgia.

Most songs about home involve motion: you're either leaving or returning, rarely actually staying there. Despite the occasional successful paean to fireside comforts (Adem's *Homesongs*) or domestic routine (Kate Bush's *Aerial*), the perils of writing about settling down are well illustrated by Crosby, Stills, Nash and Young's dreadful 'Our House'. A monument to the smugness and sanctimony of millionaire hippies, it found its true calling decades later when it appeared in a mortgage advert. Mortgage-rock – not much of a genre, is it?

Simon and Garfunkel's 'Homeward Bound' is the only rock classic written while waiting for a train at Widnes station. Inspired by the loneliness of the long-distance folk singer, it transcended life-on-the-road self-pity to resonate with all the decade's wandering souls. The touring life can give musicians empathy with other long-term absentees: New Order's 'Love Vigilantes' is narrated by a soldier on leave, who eventually makes it back to his wife and child only to discover that (spoiler warning!) he's a ghost.

To Edwin Starr, heralding his homecoming in '25 Miles' with a lusty 'Feet don't fail me now!', home is a woman. To John Denver, author of 'Take Me Home, Country Roads', it's a particular region. He sang the praises of West Virginia; Toots and the Maytals set course for West Jamaica.

When I was younger, I took Madness at face value, hearing only the broad observational humour and missing the kernel of melancholy; I blame the cheeky chappy videos. Like 'Baggy Trousers', 'Our House' uses quotidian detail to explain an adult's yearning for the simplicity of childhood: 'I remember way back then when everything was true.'

In retrospect, Blur's 'Coffee and TV' seems to presage Graham Coxon's departure from the group. Post-Britpop and post-alcoholism, the guitarist wrote and sang this farewell to all the things his former life represented: 'Sociability, it's hard enough for me / Take me away from this big bad world and agree to marry me.' Similar nesting instincts were widespread during rock's post-1960s fallout, when confusion and fragmentation inspired old-fashioned yearnings. Carole King's 'So Far Away' asks, in a mellifluous sigh of frustration, 'Doesn't anybody stay in one place anymore?'

Now for some darker interpretations. For Gil Scott-Heron's lonely junkie, a crackhouse is not a home, while Roxy Music counter

CSN&Y's hippie idyll with a desolate vision of high-end living, whether 'penthouse perfection' or 'bungalow ranch style'. Its haunting opulence and depiction of moneyed alienation must have given Radiohead some ideas. Finally, Mark Lanegan's reading of the Gun Club's 'Carry Home' makes a shadowy companion to Edwin Starr's exuberance. Exhausted and ambivalent – 'Are you still the same?' – it's redolent of Thomas Wolfe's famous maxim: You can't go home again.

THE PLAYLIST

Homeward Bound Simon and Garfunkel
Love Vigilantes New Order
25 Miles Edwin Starr
Take Me Home, Country Roads Toots and the Maytals
Our House Madness
Coffee and TV Blur
So Far Away Carole King
Home Is Where the Hatred Is Gil Scott-Heron
In Every Dream Home a Heartache Roxy Music
Carry Home Mark Lanegan

SONGS ABOUT
MONEY

(▶) 'Money can't buy you happiness, but it does bring you a more pleasant form of misery.' Woody Allen said that. 'Mo' money, mo' problems.' The Notorious BIG said that. Pop music is one of the few professions that can whisk you from having not enough money to having too much, but most listeners are rightly unconcerned with the latter quandary. Rappers get away with it because the obtaining and spending of cash is in hip-hop's DNA, but if, say, Chris Martin started wailing about mo' money and mo' problems, he'd be considerably mo' unpopular. As a rule, the more you have, the less you should sing about it. Pink Floyd's sour 'Money', like John Lennon's 'imagine no possessions', invites the response: 'Easy for you to say, pal.'

The Flying Lizards' 1979 version of 'Money (That's What I Want)' satirically anticipated the tenor of the subsequent decade. Performed by Barrett Strong or the Beatles in the early 1960s, it sounded cheerfully aspirational; here it's cold and metallic, the soundtrack to an army of men in red braces on the march. ABC dressed anti-Thatcherite rhetoric in glitzy sonic finery and affixed an ambivalent coda: 'Who wants to be a millionaire? I do! I don't!'

In the troubled, cash-strapped 1970s, money was often portrayed as a corrupting force. Like the O'Jays' equally potent 'For the Love of

Money', Funkadelic's roiling 'Funky Dollar Bill' lists the lengths to which people will go for a buck. On 'Money Money', Horace Andy works the biblical line about the root of all evil into a beautifully solemn reggae classic.

No such qualms in the R'n'B world. After TLC introduced the concept of the freeloading 'scrub' to pop's lexicon in 1999, Destiny's Child pounced on it with the efficiency of prenup lawyers, propelled by a skeletal harpsichord riff. The flipside of financial dependency is examined on the Pet Shop Boys' bottomlessly poignant 'Rent', in which a kept woman ponders the cost of living in luxury. When Neil Tennant sings 'Look at my hopes, look at my dreams, the currency we've spent', the whole meaning pivots on an ambiguous punctuation mark – should that be a comma or a colon?

The Beatles wrote several songs about money, some bitter ('Taxman'), some sweet ('Can't Buy Me Love'). Ironically, financial acrimony proved to be the final nail in their coffin. Paul McCartney turned those boardroom squabbles into a heartbreaking epitaph for both the band and the decade: 'Step on the gas and wipe that tear away.'

Now for some people with no money at all. Patti Smith offers a pulse-quickening anthem for impoverished dreamers everywhere and Bing Crosby and lyricist E.Y. Harburg voiced the impotent bewilderment of Depression-struck America, despite Crosby being one of the few Americans in 1932 who had no shortage of dimes.

Finally, some wise words in the shape of William DeVaughn's philosophical slow jam, later covered by Massive Attack and Horace Andy. Easier said than done perhaps, but it's the only financial advice you can't dispute.

THE PLAYLIST

Money (That's What I Want) The Flying Lizards

How to Be a Millionaire ABC

Funky Dollar Bill Funkadelic

Money Money Horace Andy

Bills, Bills, Bills Destiny's Child

Rent Pet Shop Boys

You Never Give Me Your Money The Beatles

Free Money Patti Smith

Brother, Can You Spare a Dime? Bing Crosby

Be Thankful for What You Got William DeVaughn

NUCLEAR WAR

▶ The possibility of nuclear annihilation first dawned on me thanks to Frankie Goes to Hollywood – specifically, the twelve-inch of 'Two Tribes', which simulated a Protect and Survive announcement with rather too much accuracy for at least one ten-year-old's liking. The fact that a dance record about nuclear war was number one for *nine weeks* in 1984 reminds you how all-pervasive that fear once was. For all its horrors, terrorism just can't torment the imagination in the same way.

Songs about nukes are almost as old as the bomb itself but they were practically mandatory during the Reagan years. UB40 turned their attentions to a problem much greater than a rat in mi kitchen on 'The Earth Dies Screaming', Prince proposed a pre-Armageddon knees-up on '1999' and Pink Floyd wallowed in radioactive hell on 'Two Suns in the Sunset'. Good grief, even China Crisis had a go. Some should have left well alone. Lists of pop's most embarrassing lyrics will forever make room for Duran Duran's 'you're about as easy as a nuclear war' and Sting's 'I hope the Russians love their children too'. Personally, I hope the Russians find Sting a pompous ass too.

Randy Newman recorded 'Political Science' in 1972 but its caustic take on America's bunker-mentality foreign policy ('They all hate us anyhow / So let's drop the big one now') suits Bush even better than it did Nixon. The comedy of Electric Six's 'Gay Bar' is considerably broader but it also ruffled feathers. In a witty response to radio programmers' qualms, the gonzo chant of 'let's start a nuclear war' was changed to 'let's make a radio edit'.

An improbable hit single, OMD's 'Enola Gay' was bouncy synth-pop about the B-29 that bombed Hiroshima: 'This kiss you gave, it's never ever gonna fade away.' For a darker reflection on the events of 6 August 1945, try 'I Come and Stand at Every Door', a poem written by Nazem Hikmet, translated and set to music by Pete Seeger, and covered, with ghostly beauty, by the Byrds. The dawn of atomic anxiety produced two mesmerisingly creepy gospel numbers which compared the Second Coming to a nuclear holocaust: 'Jesus is God's Atomic Bomb' by the Swan Silvertones and 'Jesus Hits Like an Atom Bomb' by the Pilgrim Travelers.

Can's 'Mushroom' is a nightmarish vision of a nuclear blast, closing with the sound of Damo Suzuki obsessively scatting the word *dead*. Its desiccated funk segues nicely into Yo La Tengo's version of Sun Ra's call-and-response jazz track, which enlists a chorus of children to repeat each line with unsettling nonchalance: 'Nuclear war, it's a motherfucker.' On 'Breathing' Kate Bush is a terrified survivor inhaling the fallout, 'chips of plutonium . . . twinkling in every lung'.

Finally, Charles Mingus prays that nobody drops – or indeed be-bops – a bomb on him, while satirist Tom Lehrer notes, with humour as black as a full-stop, the upside of the end of the world: 'There'll be nobody left behind to grieve.' Every mushroom cloud has a silver lining.

THE PLAYLIST

Political Science Randy Newman

Gay Bar Electric Six

Enola Gay Orchestral Manoeuvres in the Dark

I Come and Stand at Every Door The Byrds

Jesus Hits Like an Atom Bomb The Pilgrim Travelers

Mushroom Can

Nuclear War (Version 2) Yo La Tengo

Breathing Kate Bush

Oh Lord, Don't Let Them Drop That Atomic Bomb on Me Charles Mingus

We Will All Go Together When We Go Tom Lehrer

JEALOUSY

(▶) The French Renaissance writer Marguerite of Angoulême observed that 'jealousy extinguishes love'. She might have added that it's impervious to logic. In the Pet Shop Boys' 'Jealousy' or Rialto's 'Monday Morning 5:19', there's no proof that the singer's lover has strayed but the mere possibility keeps him up at night. The paranoia of the Beatles' 'Run for Your Life' was so murderous that John Lennon later disowned it and wrote a (much better) song apologising for being a jealous guy.

However, soul music is adept at casting jealousy in a sympathetic light; just listen to Stevie Wonder's devastating 'Lately'. It's impossible not to feel for the Temptations, sensing the presence of a rival, on the emotionally shattering '(I Know) I'm Losing You'. Hard, too, not to be electrified by Cornelius Grant's curtain-raising guitar riff.

The finest jealousy record of recent years might be the Killers' 'Mr Brightside'. With mounting intensity it climbs towards a kind of ecstatic masochism, every painful detail of the affair – a cigarette shared, a dress removed – stoking Brandon Flowers' obsession until he finally cries, 'open up my eager eyes'. Despite claiming that he can't look, he *wants* to know everything, like Clive Owen confronting Julia Roberts in the film *Closer*. Similarly, the Wedding Present's David

Gedge unhealthily fixates on 'a stranger's hand on my favourite dress'.

There's an unusually happy ending to 'Silhouette', a 1950s hit given the reggae treatment by Dennis Brown. Brown thinks he spies his lover with another man at a lit window but when he bangs on the door it turns out he's on the wrong street and he rushes home to embrace his blameless girlfriend. Hooray! No such luck for the paralysed Korean War veteran in 'Ruby, Don't Take Your Love to Town', vainly beseeching his wife not to get her oats from another man, but the song is still cheerier than the real-life affair which inspired it: that ended in a murder-suicide.

Homicide forms the climax of Nick Cave's updated traditional ballad 'Henry Lee', in which spurned lover P.J. Harvey (Cave's partner at the time) stabs Lee with a pen-knife and throws him in a well. Two more real-life lovers duetted on 'Suffocated Love'. Over a sickly string sample from the Chantels, Tricky mutters oblique paranoia while Martina Topley-Bird sighs, 'I know why the caged bird sings.' Yes, we're into the disturbing stuff now. Performed with chilling intensity by Nirvana and eerie relish by Leadbelly, 'Where Did You Sleep Last Night?' (also known as 'In the Pines') is a dark-as-a-mineshaft Appalachian folk song. When Leadbelly orders 'shiver for me now', you can't help but oblige.

Finally, a double helping of Elvis. Costello's 'I Want You' begins as an acoustic love song before plunging into claustrophobic psychosis, from which the listener finally emerges shuddering and gasping for air. Fortunately, here's Presley with his spirited plea for trust: exactly the same sentiments as Marguerite of Angoulême but so much easier to dance to.

THE PLAYLIST

(I Know) I'm Losing You The Temptations

Mr Brightside The Killers

My Favourite Dress The Wedding Present

Silhouette Dennis Brown

Ruby, Don't Take Your Love to Town Kenny Rogers and the First Edition

Henry Lee Nick Cave and the Bad Seeds

Suffocated Love Tricky

Where Did You Sleep Last Night? Leadbelly

I Want You Elvis Costello

Suspicious Minds Elvis Presley

EUROPE

(▶) During rock music's first decade or so, continental Europe didn't hold much appeal. Most British bands wanted to be American and most Americans were happy being American, except for a few who wished they were from Liverpool. Nobody wanted to be Belgian, except Scott Walker. He was odd like that.

In the 1970s, though, the boulevards and strasses of what Donald Rumsfeld would call 'old Europe' seized pop's imagination on a string of classic albums, usually involving either Brian Eno, David Bowie, or, in the case of *Low*, perhaps the most consciously European album ever made, both. By the early 1980s, mannered europhilia was rampant. Consider poor Ultravox. 'Vienna' was their solemn homage to *Third Man* Europe, with lovers meeting in the fog like spies, but its path to number one was blocked by a somewhat different interpretation of European cultural identity: Joe Dolce's 'Shaddup You Face'.

Your choice of city says a lot. If it's Berlin, you wear black and suck in your cheeks. If it's Paris, you drink coffee by the Seine and are probably in the Style Council. If it's Zagreb (the Fall) or Christiansands (Tricky), you're just showing off.

Along with Can and Neu!, Kraftwerk gave German pop its own

distinctive voice; 'Europe Endless' is a twinkling, evocative travelogue. Apart from Bowie, nobody exchanged America for Europe as abruptly, and successfully, as U2. *Achtung Baby* was recorded with Eno in recently reunified Berlin for maximum Euro points; the *Low*-inspired 'Zoo Station' is named after a train station in the city.

'Back in the USSR' was a surprisingly potent joke, punning on Chuck Berry's 'Back in the USA' while making a droll point about homesickness. Russians embraced it, while America's reliably barmy John Birch Society accused the Beatles of fomenting communism. Joy Division started out calling themselves Warsaw, after a track on *Low* (all roads lead to *Low*), and this razor-wire punk track kicked off their first EP.

On 'Strasbourg', named after the Germany-bordering French city that Winston Churchill anointed the capital of Europe, the excellent Rakes live out their Cold War fantasies with a spirited yelp of 'Ein, zwei, drei, vier!' 'Holland, 1945' by 1990s cult heroes Neutral Milk Hotel is a tremendously catchy, peculiarly moving expression of love for Anne Frank.

But Europe's not all about dictators, spies and bloodshed. It's about cafés and croissants and girls laughing on mopeds. Count Basie's version of 'April in Paris' is pure Euro-romance while French-Algerian singer Étienne Daho's 'Week-end à Rome' is wistful, cosmopolitan synth-pop. Saint Etienne borrowed the melody, and Daho himself, for their 1995 hit 'He's On the Phone'.

Back to Europe's colder corners for the Associates' 'White Car in Germany', which is just as good as 'Vienna' and has the advantage of a sense of humour. The lyrics are as atmospheric as they are abstruse. It's only right to end with Scott Walker's ripe, gamey rendition of Jacques Brel's 'Amsterdam'. It's just like being there, and even cheaper than easyJet.

THE PLAYLIST

Europe Endless Kraftwerk
Zoo Station U2
Back in the USSR The Beatles
Warsaw Joy Division
Strasbourg The Rakes
Holland, 1945 Neutral Milk Hotel
April in Paris Count Basie
Week-end à Rome Étienne Daho
White Car in Germany The Associates
Amsterdam Scott Walker

SONGS ABOUT
SPORT

(▶) Although I retain a soft spot for EnglandNewOrder's 1990 football World Cup anthem, official sporting songs are a dire lot. The obligatory blend of blokey camaraderie and misguided optimism is never likely to produce pop gold, so one has to look for more subtle treatments of sport. Billy Bragg's songbook is riddled with football references, chiefly 'How can you lie there and think of England when you don't even know who's in the team?' from 'Greetings to the New Brunette'; Underworld named 'Born Slippy' after a greyhound; Saint Etienne paid tribute to tennis player Conchita Martinez; Half Man Half Biscuit dreamed of owning a Dukla Prague away kit; and Black Box Recorder's John Moore mused on Henman and Rusedski at Wimbledon: 'Like true British heroes they let the whole nation down.'

We start with football. Kirsty MacColl's torrid 'England 2 Colombia 0' uses the first round of the 1998 World Cup as both backdrop and metaphor for romantic deceit, while Jorge Ben exalts an African footballer on 'Ponta de Lança Africano (Umbabarauma)'. Originally on Ben's *África Brasil* album, it's now available on a compilation, *Musica de Futebol*, which proves that Brazilians are as good at singing about football as they are at playing it. By contrast, the Fall's absurdly exciting 'Theme from Sparta FC' embraces the hooligan spirit: 'English Chelsea fan, this is your last game!'

Swiss duo Yello ensured a lifetime of royalties from inspiration-starved TV producers when they released 'The Race's brassy, tribal throb, complete with roaring engines and chattering commentary. Pop's most famous cycling enthusiasts are Kraftwerk. Their 1983 tribute to the sport's greatest race is airy and irresistible, powered by rhythmic pants of exertion. Sometimes songs simply appropriate the jargon of sport – witness Teddy Pendergrass's heartsick, boxing-themed slow jam 'Love TKO'.

On the one hand, Belle and Sebastian are the archetypal gym-shy indie bookworms; on the other, frontman Stuart Murdoch once dreamed of becoming a professional runner. That's why 'The Stars of Track and Field' is so deliciously ambivalent, poised between admiration and contempt for the school's well-toned 'beautiful people'. For my money it's the best song B&S ever wrote, containing the cherishable couplet 'Now he's throwing discus / For Liverpool and Widnes.' I've no idea what 'Take the Skinheads Bowling' is about – I'm not convinced Camper Van Beethoven knew either – but it's a classic of jingle-jangle 1980s college rock, not to mention a fine advertisement for one of the few games in which beer qualifies as a performance-enhancing drug.

Like the sport to which it refers, Roy Harper's elegiac 'When an Old Cricketer Leaves the Crease' is long and slow, but in a good way. Notable not just as the tune that John Peel said should be played at his funeral (get the hankie ready for when the colliery brass comes in) but as the only pop song to feature the phrase 'silly mid-off'. Finally, one for those refuseniks for whom sport will always signify muddy Wednesday afternoons and red-faced ogres blowing whistles: the Bonzo Dog Band's 'Sport (the Odd Boy)' even includes a sick note from mum.

THE PLAYLIST

England 2 Colombia 0 Kirsty MacColl
Ponta de Lança Africano (Umbabarauma) Jorge Ben
Theme from Sparta FC The Fall
The Race Yello
Tour de France Kraftwerk
Love TKO Teddy Pendergrass
The Stars of Track and Field Belle and Sebastian
Take the Skinheads Bowling Camper Van Beethoven
When an Old Cricketer Leaves the Crease Roy Harper
Sport (the Odd Boy) The Bonzo Dog Band

SONGS ABOUT
SIBLINGS

(▶) It's a shame Noel Gallagher insists that the mighty 'Acquiesce' is about friendship rather than his relationship with Liam. By circumstance if not by design, it's one of pop's great expressions of fraught fraternal love, capturing the way a throttlehold can rearrange itself into a hug, and vice versa.

The chemistry between siblings can be as complex and volatile as that between lovers (calm down, Liam, I'm not implying anything), but, apart from David Bowie's recurring references to schizophrenic half-brother Terry ('Aladdin Sane', 'The Bewlay Brothers', 'Jump They Say'), it's rarely examined. You're more likely to encounter erotic fascination with other people's sisters (Pulp's 'Babies') or, on a few rum occasions, the narrator's own (Palace Brothers' 'Riding', Prince's 'Sister'). 'I was only sixteen but I guess that's no excuse,' begins Prince. No, Prince. I guess not.

In the first two songs, a sister is an obstacle or a go-between. In Chris Bell's 'You and Your Sister', reimagined here with extraordinary beauty by Kim Deal and Tanya Donnelly, the lover's sister is a disapproving dragon. The Knife are a brother-sister duo, which adds another layer of intrigue to 'Pass This On's tense, steel-drum-driven electro. 'I'm in love with your brother,' Karin Dreijer confides urgently. 'You'll pass this on, won't you?'

Curtis Mayfield's 'Beautiful Brother of Mine' distinguishes the soul brother from the biological kind – 'We are not of the same seed / Although we are both the same breed' – but Marvin Gaye's 'What's Happening Brother' smudges the difference. Although it's based on the experiences of his soldier brother Frankie returning from Vietnam, the cry is universal.

Now for three brothers in trouble. Free's amiable underachiever Jake has it easy compared to the crackhead sibling of De La Soul's Posdnuos. For all the music's rainbow-hued vitality, the sense of countless chances granted and wasted is heartbreaking. Springsteen's *Nebraska* album ploughs such desolate terrain that when lawman Joe Roberts begins solemnly recounting a run-in with his bad-seed brother, it looks bad for all concerned. So here's a surprise: a moment of compassion, a second chance.

Elsewhere, plenty of siblings don't survive, whether real (the Kinks' 'Come Dancing' is a fond tribute to Ray Davies's older sister) or imagined (serpent-related tragedy stalks 'My Sister's Tiny Hands' by the Handsome Family). In the latter category, Tindersticks' 'My Sister' is a tongue-in-cheek hard-luck tale, with Stuart Staples piling misery upon misery in his lugubrious murmur. Mark 'E' Everett's loss, however, was hideously real. When his sister committed suicide in 1996, he thought back to her first attempt fourteen years earlier and wrote 'Elizabeth on the Bathroom Floor', with the startlingly weary lines: 'My name's Elizabeth / My life is piss and shit.'

Joanna Newsom uses her astrophysicist sister's words in a less grim context on the twelve-minute familial fantasia 'Emily'. In the extraordinary chorus, a disquisition on the difference between meteors, meteorites and meteoroids, one sister's scientific prose is refashioned into another's giddy poetry. Touchingly, Emily herself sings harmonies. Finally, the discotabulous Sister Sledge. They are family. They've got all their sisters with them.

THE PLAYLIST

You and Your Sister This Mortal Coil
Pass This On The Knife
What's Happening Brother Marvin Gaye
My Brother Jake Free
My Brother's a Basehead De La Soul
Highway Patrolman Bruce Springsteen
My Sister Tindersticks
Elizabeth on the Bathroom Floor Eels
Emily Joanna Newsom
We Are Family Sister Sledge

THE SUN

▶ The best thing about the British weather is that sunshine is greeted with such grateful delight. When summer finally arrives, it's as if people can't believe this astonishing entity is back in their lives and they have no idea how long it will hang around so they'd better damn well make the most of it. They act like they're witnessing a miracle.

Unreliable climates produce a certain kind of song about the sun. When the Beach Boys sang about sunshine it was a given, a daily backdrop to their lives, but George Harrison's 'Here Comes the Sun' has a northern European sense of excitement and relief: 'It seems like years since it's been here.' I think Nina Simone's version is better still. Tentative at first, then slowly flooding with warmth and wonder, it's practically a religious experience. (This whole list could be filled with equally unimpeachable 1960s classics so in the interests of variety you'll have to imagine an alternative ten comprising the likes of 'Sunny Afternoon' and 'Sunshine of Your Love'.)

Sunrise means one thing when you've woken up early and entirely another when you've stayed up late. It's a fair assumption that the Beloved weren't at the getting-up-for-a-jog end of things when they wrote 'The Sun Rising'. This pulsing house track has the soft glow of a chemical dawn. Psychedelia's obsession with the sun also had a narcotic quality but next to the head-trip intensity of Pink Floyd or Traffic, Donovan's 'Sunshine Superman', a guileless hybrid of rock, jazz and Indian music, sounds positively childlike.

A great sunny day record can warm your heart even in a blizzard and 'Automatically Sunshine' lives up to its name. Even without Diana Ross, the Supremes released some underrated Motown gems; this, from their Smokey Robinson-produced *Floy Joy* album, is one of them. Brix Smith formed the Adult Net when she left the Fall and brought us one jingly-jangly indie marvel, 'Waking Up in the Sun'. Len were a brother-and-sister Canadian group whose solitary hit cloaked angsty lyrics ('I missed a million miles of fun') in ice-cream-in-the-park jollity and became a misplaced summer classic, reaching the Top 10 in December 1999.

For some people, the sun invites a cosmic perspective. As the 1970s dawned, Charles Stepney's Rotary Connection attempted to redefine soul's dimensions with their opulent, rainbow-hued arrangements. 'I Am the Black Gold of the Sun', later covered by NuYorican Soul, was their immaculate zenith; singer Minnie Riperton sounds about ready to lift off. Two decades later, Primal Scream experienced their own epiphany in the shape of the starry-eyed space-cadet hymn 'Higher than the Sun', here in its deep-space Dub Symphony incarnation.

Must be time for sunset: specifically, Roxy Music's 'Sunset', in which Bryan Ferry waxes lyrical about 'horizon's appointment' and 'sunburst fingers'. As a counterpoint to all of the above, the Velvet Underground see us out by claiming that the sun is a giant waste of time if you're heartbroken. Bang goes their barbecue invite.

THE PLAYLIST

Here Comes the Sun Nina Simone

The Sun Rising The Beloved

Sunshine Superman Donovan

Automatically Sunshine The Supremes

Waking Up in the Sun The Adult Net

Steal My Sunshine Len

I Am the Black Gold of the Sun Rotary Connection

Higher than the Sun (A Dub Symphony in Two Parts)
   Primal Scream

Sunset Roxy Music

Who Loves the Sun The Velvet Underground

SONGS ABOUT
AMERICA

(▶) America, as Morrissey helpfully reminded us, is not the world, but it feels like it sometimes. Its influence on music, as on most things, is inescapable. You might as well try to ignore the sun.

No space, unfortunately, for the Manic Street Preachers' 'ifwhiteamericatoldthetruthforonedayit'sworldwouldfallapart' (you have to love that title, misplaced apostrophe and all), the Goats' bouncy protest rap 'Typical American' or Debbie Harry's daft but endearing 'French Kissing in the USA'. Or should that be freedom kissing? Instead, we look to the movie *Team America* and its lusty litany of the country's contributions to the world – 'Rock 'n' roll, fuck yeah! / The internet, fuck yeah! / Slavery, fuck yeah!' – encased in a flawless parody of gung-ho, Simpson-and-Bruckheimer coke-rock.

Nothing evokes the sheer size of America more eloquently than Simon and Garfunkel's miniature road movie about a couple who go 'to look for America', without knowing exactly what that means. You don't have to go looking for Britain in the same way; it's over there, just behind the Tesco superstore. REM's first national tour inspired their own, more oblique travelogue, named after a chain of gas stations, and full of cryptic references to mad Roman emperors. The line 'Jefferson I think we're lost' doubles as a simple remark to their manager Jefferson Holt and a cry for help to one of America's founding fathers.

On their Vietnam-era hit 'American Woman', Canadian group the Guess Who thinly disguised their scorn for Nixon's America as a break-up song; the line 'I don't need your war machines' gives the game away somewhat. Next to 'I'm So Bored with the USA', it sounds like a masterclass in subtlety. Lyrically, this wasn't the Clash's finest hour but there's something magnificently adolescent about declaring the world's most powerful country *boring*. Kim Wilde, on the other hand, envisioned America as some kind of all-singing, all-dancing utopia on her never-bettered debut single.

In the west, at least, most so-called anti-Americans love as many things about the US as they hate. Their anthem should be 'Democracy', Leonard Cohen's biting but even-handed lament for 'the cradle of the best and of the worst'. As Cohen growls, 'I love the country but I can't stand the scene.' 'Born in the USA' must be pop's most misunderstood song – Ronald Reagan embraced it and one cloth-eared conservative pundit deemed it 'a grand, cheerful affirmation' – but what did Springsteen expect? If you're going to write a song about traumatised Vietnam veterans, don't make it sound like you're about to bomb Cambodia. This sparse demo version, originally intended for the *Nebraska* album, is how the song should be heard.

The last two songs both emerged out of irritation with Irving Berlin's 'God Bless America'. In 1971, Swamp Dogg, the soul genius that time forgot, asked 'God Bless America for What?' His record label shamefully copped out by omitting the title's last two words from the album sleeve. Three decades earlier, Woody Guthrie offered a defiant, class-conscious, yet still stirring version of patriotism on 'This Land Is Your Land': 'This land was made for you and me.'

THE PLAYLIST

America, Fuck Yeah Team America

America Simon and Garfunkel

Little America REM

American Woman The Guess Who

I'm So Bored with the USA The Clash

Kids in America Kim Wilde

Democracy Leonard Cohen

Born in the USA (demo version) Bruce Springsteen

God Bless America for What? Swamp Dogg

This Land Is Your Land Woody Guthrie

LONDON

(▶) London casts a spell over songwriters' imaginations to an extent rivalled only by New York. Like singing Peter Ackroyds, they devote whole albums to charting the capital's psychogeography: think Blur's *Parklife*, the Libertines' *Up the Bracket* or the Sabres of Paradise's lost classic *Haunted Dancehall*. For others, a brief mention will suffice, like the Thameside peregrinations that introduce the Verve's 'History' or the Clapham Common rendezvous in Squeeze's 'Up the Junction'. London's geography provides a kind of shorthand: Chelsea stands for trendy vapidity (Elvis Costello), Dalston for demimonde drama (Razorlight). All human life is here.

Calypso star Lord Kitchener arrived in London in 1948 on the *Empire Windrush*, as one of the first wave of Trinidadian immigrants. 'London is the Place for Me', composed on board the ship, bubbles with enthusiasm for his new home. Lily Allen offers a more bittersweet perspective, taking in the sights from lunching nine-to-fivers to pimps and muggers. While the verses ponder the dark side, the chorus stakes its claim to heatwave ubiquity: 'Sun is in the sky, oh why, oh why would I want to be anywhere else?'

Outsiders often have the sharpest eye for London's pleasures and pitfalls: the Pogues, Pet Shop Boys and Pulp to name just three. Here are two songs mentioning trains at Euston, one arriving, one leaving. Morrissey stands on a station platform taunting a departing Mancunian (himself?), 'Do you think you've made the right decision this time?' Like a female Jarvis Cocker, Catatonia's Cerys Matthews stuffed herself with Britpop celebrity until it made her sick. 'Londinium', written by bandmate Mark Roberts, is an angry farewell to the 'neon disease' and 'poison Thames'. Anyone who grumbles that the capital is overrated will enjoy the line 'I come alive outside the M25.'

Woking-born Paul Weller grew up far enough outside the city to view it with fascination and just a touch of fear, the latter coursing through this vivid nightmare of a subway beating in the days long before Oyster cards. Carter USM also evoked public-transport peril on '24 Minutes to Tulse Hill' but here's an alternative London-based pun on an American song. Playing off Simon and Garfunkel's 'The Only Living Boy in New York', it's a moist-eyed rallying cry for youth tribes and AIDS victims in the insalubrious south London district where I spent my teenage weekends.

Time for some more idyllic reflections. Taken from *Foxbase Alpha*, Saint Etienne's extended valentine to the capital, the gauzy daydream of 'London Belongs to Me' traces a summer's walk from Camden tube to the willow trees in Regent's Park. Meanwhile, John and Beverley Martyn head for Primrose Hill to watch the sunset in escapist jazz-pop style.

Off to the dark-blue stretch of the Monopoly board, where a lovestruck Vera Lynn hallucinates a city in which angels dine at the Ritz and the streets are paved with stars, and then south of the river, where Ray Davies surveys the hurly-burly from his high-rise solitude. As eloquent and moving as any song ever written, 'Waterloo Sunset' requires no elaboration from me. Just listen to it.

THE PLAYLIST

London is the Place for Me Lord Kitchener

LDN Lily Allen

London The Smiths

Londinium Catatonia

Down in the Tube Station at Midnight The Jam

The Only Living Boy in New Cross Carter the Unstoppable Sex Machine

London Belongs to Me Saint Etienne

Primrose Hill John and Beverley Martyn

A Nightingale Sang in Berkeley Square Vera Lynn

Waterloo Sunset The Kinks

STORYTELLING
SONGS

(▶) As a kid, I was a sucker for a story song, especially if it reminded me of *The Twilight Zone*. I once held the belief, since revised, that the best album ever made was Jeff Wayne's *War of the Worlds* and still have a soft spot for 'Camouflage', Stan Ridgway's account of a life-saving US marine who turns out to be – take that, M Night Shyamalan! – a ghost.

From medieval troubadours to the Streets, a good narrative casts a spell. It's interesting how many storytelling songs end in tears. During pop's pre-Beatles infancy, a whole genre was devoted to tales of teenage love cut brutally short: the death disc. As morbid and melodramatic as a public information film, the best tended to involve brooding bikers with poor road safety skills. Watch out, the Leader of the Pack! Oops, too late. Al Wilson's 'The Snake' is even crueller. This soul stomper, which punctuates each narrative step with a vaulting chord change, tells of a woman who unwisely nurses a snake back to health: '"Ah, shut up, silly woman!" said that reptile with a grin / "You knew darn well I was a snake before you brought me in."'

Love is the only fatality in Squeeze's kitchen-sink classic 'Up the Junction', which deftly chronicles an entire relationship, from first meeting to booze-sodden collapse, in just over three minutes. Bob Dylan's melodically repetitive songs, accruing layers of significance like a canvas accumulates layers of paint, are perfect for storytelling. 'Lily, Rosemary and the Jack of Hearts' builds up so much detail and drama over its nine minutes that it could almost be adapted into a screenplay.

Back to the morgue with two suicide songs. Even Bobbie Gentry couldn't explain why poor Billie Joe jumped off the Tallahatchie bridge in her country gothic masterpiece; she contended that the real story was the callous matter-of-factness of his girlfriend's family. The heroine of Hot Chocolate's uncommonly bleak 'Emma' was considerate enough to leave a note, blaming her thwarted dreams of stardom. Seems that not everyone's a winner, babe.

Politicised soul stars used stories to dramatise inner-city strife. Curtis Mayfield had 'Billy Jack'; Stevie Wonder gave us 'Living for the City', a would-be rags-to-riches journey in which the riches prove crushingly elusive. Hip-hop inherited the urban drama, if rarely the compassion, and one of the genre's finest narrators is Ghostface Killah. Influenced more by the screen than the page, here he mounts a dense, visceral onslaught of shifting tenses, fragmented dialogue and razor-sharp detail. When the action reaches a bloody peak, he teases, 'To be continued . . .'

In the body count stakes, hip-hop is rivalled by folk. In 'Matty Groves', Fairport Convention's radical, exquisitely told take on a traditional murder ballad, a rural affair culminates in a double slaying. Finally, 'The Mariner's Revenge Song' is a 21st-century composition that sounds much older, a gleefully lurid potboiler of high-seas score-settling that's half Edgar Allan Poe shocker, half Kurt Weill operetta. As with all great story songs, you're desperate to hear how it ends.

THE PLAYLIST

Leader of the Pack The Shangri-Las

The Snake Al Wilson

Up the Junction Squeeze

Lily, Rosemary and the Jack of Hearts Bob Dylan

Ode to Billie Joe Bobbie Gentry

Emma Hot Chocolate

Living for the City Stevie Wonder

Shakey Dog Ghostface Killah

Matty Groves Fairport Convention

The Mariner's Revenge Song The Decemberists

NAMED AFTER WOMEN

(▶) Most Marthas fondly remember the first time they heard 'Martha My Dear', most Lucys feel strangely flattered when they discover 'Lucy in the Sky with Diamonds', and anyone called Delilah must have a soft spot for Tom Jones. But some titles are misleading. The protagonists of Scott Walker's 'Jackie' and Blur's 'Tracy Jacks' are men, and, at the risk of spoiling the twist for anyone who hasn't heard it yet, so is the Kinks' 'Lola'.

We open with the Turtles' winning summary of teenage love under fire: 'Your looks intoxicate me / Even though your folks hate me.' Like the same band's 'Happy Together', 'Elenore' has a teasing wisp of a verse and a great surging moon-launch of a chorus. A Tribe Called Quest's Q-Tip woos *his* dream woman with sauntering confidence ('If you need 'em I got crazy prophylactics') and, on this remix, the bobbing beachfront groove from Carly Simon's 'Why'.

Those crazy prophylactics would have helped Michael Jackson avoid the clutches of Billie Jean. For years, seduced by Jackson's anguished protestations and that addictive, panther-like bassline, I assumed Billie Jean was a stalker, but now I wonder: maybe the pop star doth protest too much and the kid really *was* his son. Producer Quincy Jones, worried that people would think it was about tennis player Billie Jean King, nearly changed the title to 'Not My Lover'. Jackson, and wisdom, prevailed.

I love the way that, unlike the boomingly confident Temptations, Four Tops frontman Levi Stubbs sang with a gulp of desperation, as if he were only one verse away from meltdown. 'Bernadette' is a fraught peak – when Stubbs cries 'Bernadette!' he sounds like someone standing in the middle of the road, screaming at the back of a departing taxi. The melodrama continues with 'Eloise', originally a fluke 1968 hit for Barry Ryan and beefed up eighteen years later by the Damned. Both versions are hammy – more William Shatner than Scott Walker – but joyously so.

'Marian's sonorous mausoleum ambience is the quintessence of goth – you just know that the woman in question is ivory of skin, ebony of hair and tight of bodice. The Sisters of Mercy once recorded a terrific, scenery-chewing rendition of 'Jolene', but Dolly Parton's original requires no embellishment. Sung from a position of terrifying powerlessness, it's a wrenching twist on the break-up song tradition, anticipating the calamity before it's even happened. Elvis Costello greets a now-married ex-girlfriend with barbed compassion on 'Alison'. The knife-twisting message: *You should have stuck with me.*

'Angie', the Rolling Stones' wearily resigned 1970s ballad, was named after (although not written about) Keith Richards's baby daughter, Angela. You can only marvel at the stupidity of the German wonks who hijacked it as Angela Merkel's unofficial election theme in 2005.

As campaign messages go, 'All the dreams we held so close seemed to all go up in smoke' isn't a classic. Bob Dylan wrote 'Sara' in 1976 for his soon-to-be-ex-wife, Sara Lownds. His lifelong talent for obfuscation makes this flash of uncommon frankness all the more arresting: 'Stayin' up for days in the Chelsea Hotel / Writin' "Sad-Eyed Lady of the Lowlands" for you.'

THE PLAYLIST

Elenore The Turtles
Bonita Applebum (12" Why version) A Tribe Called Quest
Billie Jean Michael Jackson
Bernadette The Four Tops
Eloise The Damned
Marian The Sisters of Mercy
Jolene Dolly Parton
Alison Elvis Costello
Angie The Rolling Stones
Sara Bob Dylan

NAMED AFTER MEN

(▶) Any expectant parent will tell you that choosing a name for a boy is harder than it is for a girl. Songwriters face a similar quandary. Look around your friends and workmates and it's likely that most of the women's names would make serviceable song titles – many already have – while most of the men's would fall flat. One tends towards poetry, the other, prose. There is not a single man's name (well, not a single Anglo-American one) as intrinsically musical as, say, Emily. Small wonder that most musicians favour the richer cadences of a full name (the Coral's 'Simon Diamond'), the extra weight of a famous one (Dylan's 'John Wesley Harding') or the glamour of an exotic one (Abba's 'Fernando').

My admiration for Jacques Brel's (and Scott Walker's) 'Jackie' is unwavering, but here's a compelling alternative. Sinéad O'Connor's Jackie is a long-dead sailor whose equally deceased lover still haunts the shores, awaiting his return. She makes such a convincing wraith that you may feel the need to exorcise your speakers afterwards. The Supremes' AWOL paramour doesn't have the excuse of being lost at sea. If he ever comes home, Nathan Jones is due an almighty ear-bashing.

A famous name packs a punch even if you can't work out what it's doing there. What does the twisted optimism of Gorillaz' dubwise hip-hop have to do with the leather-faced former mayor of Carmel? Search me. But the second Gorillaz album continued the theme with 'Dirty Harry'; fingers crossed for the appropriately simian 'Every Which Way But Loose' next time. More explicably, Scritti Politti's Green Gartside invokes Jacques Derrida for his arch musings on capitalism and desire. Pretentious? *Peut-être un peu.*

Now for two names that won't be challenging the playground dominance of Jack any time soon. Aaron Neville is 'ducking rocks, catching stones' on the loping survivalist funk of 'Hercules', while Donovan concocts a whimsical, only-in-1969 fantasia about a psychedelic shaman called Barabajagal, redeeming the tweeness of the lyrics with the fried, filthy energy of the groove.

Simon and Garfunkel's Richard Cory is a 19th-century David Watts: rich, charming, immaculate. You can see why Paul Simon's struggling wage slave envies Cory's wealth and 'the orgies on his yacht' (an orgy! On a yacht!), but even when Cory puts a bullet in his own head, the chorus doesn't change – the narrator still thinks the rich man's got the better deal. Only marginally less forlorn is the beaten and bowed little boy in Suzanne Vega's 'Luka'.

'Johnny B Goode' is the quintessential example of self-mythologising rock 'n' roll, covered by the thin cloak of an alias. Go, Chuck, go! Midlake's 'Roscoe' is a much stranger alter ego: the manly, wood-chopping hero of an agrarian daydream. 'What if my name had changed into something more productive like Roscoe?' ponders the unproductively named Tim Smith. 'Been born in 1891?' Coloured by the music's otherworldly magic, it sounds like a perfectly sensible scenario.

THE PLAYLIST

Jackie Sinéad O'Connor

Nathan Jones The Supremes

Clint Eastwood Gorillaz

Jacques Derrida Scritti Politti

Hercules Aaron Neville

Barabajagal Donovan

Richard Cory Simon and Garfunkel

Luka Suzanne Vega

Johnny B Goode Chuck Berry

Roscoe Midlake

DREAMS

(▶) I've always fancied beginning an article with Prince's disclaimer from '1999' ('I was dreaming when I wrote this / Forgive me if it goes astray') but, not being Prince, I doubt I could get away with it. Of course, '1999' doesn't go astray at all. Like many songs which reference dreams, it has no dream-like qualities. Here, I'm looking for more revealing treatments of the theme.

How strange it must have been in 1968 to hear the Mamas and the Papas, key players on the LA scene, bow out with a respectfully covered 1930s ditty about sweet dreams and sunbeams. How effortlessly uplifting it still sounds. Metallica's 'Enter Sandman' can make even heavy metal haters instinctively configure their fingers into devil's horns. It's rock music as imagined by Wes Craven, James Hetfield savouring his monster-under-the-bed growl while guitarist Kirk Hammett chops away like a mad axeman. Metallica aren't exactly renowned for their sense of humour but this strikes me as a very funny record.

While Metallica dwell on a child's night terrors, the Small Faces take a whimsical euphemism for bedtime down the psychedelic rabbit hole. It hails from an era when even records that weren't metaphors for hallucinogens sounded like metaphors for hallucinogens: 'When you're slipping into sleep / There's a world you will find / That's all yours.' On the Electric Prunes' garage-psych classic, recently reissued on the *Nuggets* compilation, the nocturnal vision of a lover's presence is so convincing that the dreamer wakes up traumatised.

The Gunter Kallmann Choir's oft-sampled 'Daydream' has a magical, idyllic verse and a dreadfully twee chorus. Bizarro-pop duo I Monster keep the best bit and splice it with a robot voice gurgling: 'I dream a dirty dream of you baby / You're crawling on the bathroom floor.' Somehow it's charming enough to feature on adverts and chillout compilations while being uncomfortably evocative of a psychotic episode. It's rare that Nico's tombstone tonsils can be described as comforting but this Lou Reed-penned lullaby, named after a Sinatra song, casts a reassuring spell.

The next three tracks all describe specific nocturnal visions. John Holt witters entertainingly about Ali Baba, *Alice in Wonderland* and the three blind mice. 'Dreaming of the Queen' has the authentic illogic of a dream, with improbable celebrity encounters and embarrassing public nudity. Neil Tennant wrote it in 1993, envisaging it as the dream of someone who fears he has AIDS, hence Princess Diana's heartbreaking lines, 'There were no more lovers left alive / And that's why love has died.' Four years later, they acquired a whole different meaning.

A queen also figures in the next song. In 1969, Neil Young offered to write the soundtrack for an apocalyptic screenplay, *After the Gold Rush*, written by actor Dean Stockwell. The film was never made but its influence shaped this bizarrely moving vision of knights in armour, spaceships and ecological disaster. Finally, the Smiths take a conceit that goes back to Bobby Darin's 'Dream Lover' and beyond – lonely guy only finds love in his sleep – and elevate it to operatic heights. Sweet dreams.

THE PLAYLIST

Dream a Little Dream of Me The Mamas and the Papas
Enter Sandman Metallica
Up the Wooden Hills to Bedfordshire The Small Faces
I Had Too Much to Dream Last Night The Electric Prunes
Daydream in Blue I Monster
Wrap Your Troubles in Dreams Nico
Ali Baba John Holt
Dreaming of the Queen Pet Shop Boys
After the Gold Rush Neil Young
Last Night I Dreamt That Somebody Loved Me The Smiths

SHORT
SONGS

(▶) There is something primal about a song lasting less than two minutes. The short song flourished when rock 'n' roll was young and in a hurry, like the people who made it. It resurfaces whenever bands crave simplicity. No frills or fuss. Garage-rock in the 1960s. Punk in the 1970s. Hardcore in the 1980s. Japanese noise-rock in the '90s. Most recently, the White Stripes managed it with 'Fell in Love with a Girl'. Short songs tend to value velocity.

Some are jokes. The Dead Kennedys' 'Short Songs' repeats the line 'I like short songs' thirteen times. The world's briefest single, a double A-side, contained Napalm Death's 'You Suffer' and the Electro Hippies' 'Mega Armageddon Death'. Two tracks, one second apiece. Ho ho. But a good short song isn't a gimmick. It just doesn't waste any time. It's a test of discipline and songwriting craft. It's also a kind of prison. Ambitious songwriters need space. Even Wire and the Minutemen, bastions of brevity, couldn't stay hemmed in for ever.

Short songs make good intros and outros. Brian Wilson wrote 'Our Prayer' in 1967 to open *Smile*. Surfers singing like Gregorian monks. Pop as sacrament. It's the album's philosophy in a nutshell.

Which 1950s classic to choose? 'That's All Right Mama'? 'Rave On'? How about 'Summertime Blues'? It's one second shy of two minutes. Teenage kicks, 1959 vintage.

Art-school punks Wire scorned needless repetition. 'It was a process of elimination,' explained singer Colin Newman. Their *Pink Flag* album contained twenty-one punk haikus. Here's the briefest. A brisk attack on life-wrecking tabloid exposés in twenty-eight seconds. US hardcore bands worshipped Wire. So did Elastica. They even 'borrowed' their melodies. This one is theirs alone though. A quickie about quickies. The Pixies made compact songs which writhed with ideas. Incest, mutilation and Frank Black's crazed yelp whizz past on 'Broken Face'.

It can't all be punk blurts. Here's a small interlude from a big band. It comes from Duke Ellington's Shakespeare-inspired *Such Sweet Thunder* album. (Hank Cinq is Henry V's jazz name.) This is good for those who find that a little jazz goes a long way. If you're sharp, you can tell a story in two minutes. Take the Mountain Goats' 'Dance Music' (divorce) or Syd Barrett's 'Effervescing Elephant' (an effervescing elephant). On 'Frank's Wild Years' Tom Waits gives his character a past, a future, a plot, a motive. He makes Raymond Carver look like a windbag. Frank later got a whole concept album to himself. It wasn't necessary.

Most punks made minimalism taut and punchy. Cardiff's Young Marble Giants made it spacious and spooky. 'Final Day' is a nuclear lullaby. A pocket apocalypse. When it ends, it demands to be played again. The Magnetic Fields' *69 Love Songs* album does what it says on the tin. Some are leisurely, some abrupt. 'Very Funny' offers a painful glimpse of infidelity. Dudley Klute stops singing because he sounds too forlorn to continue.

Dance music loathes economy. A decent groove needs time. But away from the dancefloor, electronic interludes thrive. Try this one from the Aphex Twin. Breezy pizzicato strings, a gentle bass hum, a plangent keyboard melody. Pure bliss. So there you go. Ten songs. Just shy of fifteen minutes. All dispatched in short sentences. Like this one.

THE PLAYLIST

Our Prayer The Beach Boys
Summertime Blues Eddie Cochran
Field Day for the Sundays Wire
Vaseline Elastica
Broken Face Pixies
Sonnet to Hank Cinq Duke Ellington
Frank's Wild Years Tom Waits
Final Day Young Marble Giants
Very Funny The Magnetic Fields
Goon Gumpas Aphex Twin

LONG
SONGS

(▶) When I was a teenager, easily swayed by Jesus and Mary Chain interviews, I decided that no song needed to be longer than four minutes – maybe five, tops. I soon changed my mind, but while doing battle with Jethro Tull's preposterous 'Thick as a Brick' in the interests of research, I remembered my old opposition to musical obesity.

Of course it's all subjective. You can lose yourself in a long song (we're talking nine minutes plus) or simply lose patience. Personally, I find myself checking my watch long before 'Rapper's Delight' or 'Sad-Eyed Lady of the Lowlands' have concluded their business. The most honestly titled song I've ever come across is Daft Punk's 'Too Long'. Of those that reward your patience, it pained me to omit Lou Reed's 'Street Hassle', Bowie's 'Station to Station', Can, Mogwai, Sigur Rós and more soul, disco and electronic music than I could possibly list.

Donna Summer's 'I Feel Love', elongated to almost sixteen minutes by Patrick Cowley, is one of dance music's urtexts: glittering testament to the ecstasy of repetition. I like to think that there's some parallel universe in which it never ends. The influence of krautrock on song structure is incalculable, from Can's busy, humid jams to Neu!'s airy proto-techno. The first track on Neu!'s first album, 'Hallogallo' launched their career with a gravity-defying rush.

The Stone Roses once admitted that they based 'Fools Gold' on Can's 'I'm So Green'. This writhing, mantric, ceaselessly engaging groove justifies the band's reputation more than anything on their debut album. Fela Kuti conjured up his own vision of funk, weaving jazz and African rhythms into enthrallingly rich compositions such as 'He Miss Road'. Underworld have a genius for arrangement, marrying impressionistic songwriting to techno's nocturnal pulse. Listening to 'Dirty Epic' feels like watching London (or Tokyo, or New York) unfurl through the window of a speeding night-time cab.

Long songs often confound genre labels. If the sepulchral clatter of 'Bela Lugosi's Dead' is goth, then it's unlike any other goth song before or since. It's more as if dub had been hatched in Transylvania rather than Jamaica. Television emerged from New York punk but loved psychedelia's wide open spaces so much that when Lester Bangs first saw them play he wailed, 'This is just San Francisco all over again!' 'Marquee Moon' still sounds wild and revelatory. Fairport Convention's 'A Sailor's Life' is a traditional folk ballad that gallops off into psychedelic pastures.

Some landmark epics leave you feeling that all bets are off. Recorded in one take, 'Sister Ray' translated the Velvet Underground's toxic personal chemistry into blistering noise. It sounds like a revolution, or a war. Lou Reed and John Cale aren't so much jamming here as trying to kill each other with sound. After that our ears need a rest, in the form of Tortoise's twenty-one-minute jazz-dub-indie-krautrock opus 'DJed'. So that's a ten-song playlist that lasts over two hours. Time for some Jesus and Mary Chain.

THE PLAYLIST

I Feel Love (Patrick Cowley Remix) Donna Summer

Hallogallo Neu!

Fools Gold 9.53 The Stone Roses

He Miss Road Fela Kuti and the Africa 70

Dirty Epic Underworld

Bela Lugosi's Dead Bauhaus

Marquee Moon Television

A Sailor's Life Fairport Convention

Sister Ray The Velvet Underground

DJed Tortoise

CRYING

(▶) In his 1986 song 'Levi Stubbs' Tears', Billy Bragg nailed the power of music to make you feel less alone, with reference to the Four Tops' famously lachrymose frontman: 'When the world falls apart some things stay in place / Levi Stubbs' tears run down his face.' It's why we are drawn to songs about crying. Someone sobbing in an otherwise silent room is one of the worst sounds in the world. A quivery voice backed by the Motown house band, on the other hand, is cathartic.

We have two 'Cry Me a River's to choose from. Same title, same sentiments. Justin Timberlake has malevolent charm on his side but Julie London's breezy vengefulness wins the day. She sounds like a nice girl whose emotional wounds have hardened into a thick, impermeable scab. Revenge also motivates ? and the Mysterians' deceptively perky garage-rock classic. As for that weirdly precise title, it was changed from the more risqué '69 Tears' for fear of offending radio programmers.

Boys, as the Cure averred, don't cry. Or rather, they do but they make a big deal about not showing it. Smokey Robinson was king of Motown's stiff-upper-lip school with 'Tears of a Clown' and 'Tracks of My Tears'. Nobody else could make putting on a brave face sound so heroic. The Kinks' 'Stop Your Sobbing' was a so-so ballad until the Pretenders flipped the protagonists' genders and gave it a pungent kick. Chrissie Hynde's target sounds like a bit of a sap but even the blokiest blokes cry sometimes. The key to Mike Skinner's 'Dry Your Eyes' is that 'mate' in the chorus: the equivalent of a manly, back-patting hug followed by a consoling pint.

The Rolling Stones wrote the beautiful 'As Tears Go By' to kickstart the career of Mick Jagger's girlfriend Marianne Faithfull. Mission accomplished. What strikes the listener now is how jaded it sounds for songwriters barely into their twenties and a singer not yet nineteen: the hollowed-out rich girl softly weeping as she watches children play, her own youth already over. Chic's reputation rests on their peerless disco floor-fillers but they could write a potent ballad too. 'Will You Cry' is their attempt at a self-fulfilling prophecy, a song designed to tweak a dastardly ex-lover's conscience and tear ducts.

Obeying the principle that nothing says weepie quite like a string section, Tindersticks' 'Tiny Tears' has a deadly elegance. As Stuart Staples addresses someone preparing to break his girlfriend's heart, he sounds like an accusing phantom, roaming the earth making people feel shit about themselves. Massive Attack's 'Teardrop' is one of those tracks that puts the chill in chillout. Never mind what Elizabeth Fraser's elliptical lyrics about a 'teardrop on the fire' actually mean; the amniotic pulse and the dread clang of piano speak volumes. Finally, Roy Orbison's 'Crying' is edged out by Rebekah Del Rio's *a cappella*, Spanish-language version from *Mulholland Drive*. In the film, Del Rio collapses on stage while the song continues, disembodied. There's not a dry eye in the house.

THE PLAYLIST

Cry Me a River Julie London
96 Tears ? and the Mysterians
Tracks of My Tears Smokey Robinson and the Miracles
Stop Your Sobbing The Pretenders
Dry Your Eyes The Streets
As Tears Go By Marianne Faithfull
Will You Cry (When You Hear This Song) Chic
Tiny Tears Tindersticks
Teardrop Massive Attack
Llorando (Crying) Rebekah Del Rio

HEAVEN AND HELL

(▶) As a devout non-believer, I subscribe to the philosophy of Norman Whitfield's 'You Make Your Own Heaven and Hell Right Here on Earth', but even Richard Dawkins would have to concede that belief in those great unknowns has been good for music. Whether they are as whimsically presented as the heaven in Amen Corner's '(If Paradise Is) Half as Nice' or as frighteningly tangible as the hell hound on Robert Johnson's trail, these concepts raise the stakes.

We should start off in hell and work our way up. The Reverend A.W. Nix was a 1920s hellfire preacher intent on terrifying Americans onto the path of virtue with gospel-influenced sermons such as the Yuletide-ruining 'Death Might Be Your Christmas Gift'. Here he describes, with thunderous relish, the progress of a Hades-bound train collecting those benighted souls foolish enough not to heed the words of the Reverend A.W. Nix.

That flows thrillingly into the titular chimes of AC/DC's 'Hells Bells', the kind of solemnly ridiculous metal monster for which the devil's horns salute was invented. Doubtless the Reverend would have taken a dim view of AC/DC, but I suspect he would have warmed to 'Lake of Fire'. When I heard Nirvana's version, I assumed they'd dusted down something from the 1930s, but it was written in 1984 by

Curt Kirkwood, an Arizonan who knew his way around the scorched terrain of old-time religion. His band's howlingly raw recording anticipates not just Nirvana but also the White Stripes.

The language of hell also fuels songs of ghetto outrage. Curtis Mayfield whips up a righteous storm on the infernally funky 'Don't Worry (If There's a Hell Below We're All Going to Go)', while the Wu-Tang Clan's Raekwon and Ghostface paint their corner of Staten Island as a lurid warzone: 'What do you believe in? Heaven or hell? / You don't believe in heaven cuz we're livin' in hell.'

Only someone as immersed in scripture as Nick Cave could have written 'Mutiny in Heaven', which reimagines the fall of Lucifer as a junkie's fever dream. As with many Birthday Party songs, Cave sounds like he recorded it while scraping cockroaches off his skin with a rusty spoon. Time to ascend to soft-rock Valhalla with Belinda Carlisle. Sampled by Orbital in their live sets, that first *a cappella* chorus still raises goosebumps. Another similarly themed 1980s hit is 'Just Like Heaven'. The scuffed-up Dinosaur Jr version is fine, but the Cure's original strikes the right note of pristine vulnerability.

Bob Dylan winks towards his earlier song about heaven and doors, not to mention several gospel and country lyrics, on his footsore travelogue 'Tryin' to Get to Heaven' ('before they close the door'). And so we end up at the place itself, with some ambivalent post-punk theology from David Byrne. His paradise, a state of divine tedium where his favourite song and the perfect kiss are on an endless loop, sounds like a kind of perdition. At least it beats taking the Black Diamond Express.

THE PLAYLIST

Black Diamond Express to Hell Part 1 Rev. A.W. Nix

Hells Bells AC/DC

Lake of Fire Meat Puppets

Don't Worry (If There's a Hell Below We're All Going to Go) Curtis Mayfield

Heaven and Hell Raekwon

Mutiny in Heaven The Birthday Party

Heaven Is a Place on Earth Belinda Carlisle

Just Like Heaven The Cure

Tryin' to Get to Heaven Bob Dylan

Heaven Talking Heads

SONGS ABOUT
GETTING OLDER

(▶) Seems you're never too young to start feeling old. Bob Dylan was just twenty-two when he cast a glum eye over his dwindled youth in 'Bob Dylan's Dream'. The Buzzcocks felt past it at twenty-one in the song 'Sixteen'. Songwriters like Paul Simon and Nicky Wire have long been preoccupied with senescence. 'How terribly strange to be seventy,' sighed Simon in 'Old Friends'.

Almost nobody sings about looking forward to getting older, preferring to look back on some misty Eden when they were young and free and all that jazz. The nostalgia gene is so strong that it takes courage to declare, as Mark E. Smith does on the Fall's 'Bill Is Dead', 'These are the greatest times of my life.' Even if they're not, chances are you'll look back in ten years' time and tell yourself they were.

We'll start by taking the long view. Ervin Drake's 'It Was a Very Good Year' is the perfect midlife song: reflective but optimistic, fond of the past rather than imprisoned by it. This version, recorded by a fifty-year-old Sinatra for his *September of My Years* album, is a titanic performance.

In the heyday of the teenager, the Beach Boys' *Pet Sounds* began with a peculiar wish: 'Wouldn't it be nice if we were older.' Here's

Brian Wilson musing again on impending maturity while his bandmates cheerfully reel off the years like ticker tape. Meanwhile, youth's already over for the twenty-one-year-old Marc Almond on Soft Cell's enervated electronic torch song.

Every record buff should hear 'Losing My Edge': frighteningly accurate electro-punk satire about somebody who has invested his entire identity in his bleeding-edge music taste only to realise one day that he's no longer the hippest kid on the block. The age gap yawns again on Steely Dan's 'Hey 19', as a sagging boomer finds his cultural references are lost on the teenager he's wooing. The music is as oily and repellent as the narrator, but then I find all Steely Dan's music oily and repellent so the effect may be unintentional. Billy Bragg is philosophical – elated, even – about encroaching middle age on 'Brickbat': 'I used to want to plant bombs at the last night of the Proms / Now you'll find me with the baby in the bathroom.'

So we arrive at old age. I reckon Neil Hannon's Scott Walkeresque study of a long-faded society girl is his masterpiece: witty, humane, unbearably moving. Almost as good is Pulp's 'Help the Aged'. Deceptively twee at first, it ascends to a cry of rage against the dimming of the light. Townes Van Zandt's 'Waiting Around to Die' could be retitled 'It Was a Very Bad Year', brutally detailing each step of a life so hopeless that the final appearance of codeine addiction comes as light relief.

Let Dusty sing us out with Goffin and King's classic about stripping away some of adulthood's layers: 'Thinking young and growing older is no sin.' It's a fine sentiment to end on.

THE PLAYLIST

It Was a Very Good Year Frank Sinatra

When I Grow Up (to Be a Man) The Beach Boys

Youth Soft Cell

Losing My Edge LCD Soundsystem

Hey 19 Steely Dan

Brickbat Billy Bragg

A Lady of a Certain Age The Divine Comedy

Help the Aged Pulp

Waiting Around to Die Townes Van Zandt

Goin' Back Dusty Springfield

LIST
SONGS

(▶) In the 1940s, list songs such as 'These Foolish Things' and 'They Can't Take That Away from Me' were urbane affairs, delivered with the suave self-assurance of a waiter at the Ritz-Carlton informing diners of the night's specials. Thanks to Dylan's 'Subterranean Homesick Blues', more recent examples tend to rattle along at the pace of an auctioneer, or a machine-gunner. The best examples of this strange genre are somewhere between exhilarating and overwhelming.

Most list songs carry the whiff of novelty, but only a few are deliberately funny. In that category, Tom Lehrer's ever-so-slightly-smug Harvard party piece 'The Elements' loses out to the Bonzo Dog Band's enduringly funny spoof of band leader introductions, in which each instrument is played by an implausible public figure: 'looking very relaxed, Adolf Hitler on vibes'.

Apart from the single word *and*, Queens of the Stone Age's salute to stimulants is nothing *but* a list, performed with the zeal of men who know whereof they speak. Poet and author Jim Carroll began his on-off music career in 1980 with this ferocious litany of punk-era New Yorkers who kicked the bucket, mostly, it must be said, from doing the stuff that Queens of the Stone Age were just singing about.

Like teenagers doodling band names on their exercise books, musicians like to acknowledge their inspirations, from high art ('Endless Art' by A House) to house music (Daft Punk's 'Teachers'). On 'Hot Topic', feminist punks Le Tigre chant a roll call of female icons in the style of a 1960s dance-craze record. Meanwhile, Pop Will Eat Itself shake out the contents of a certain kind of twentysomething man's brain: comic books, pop and telly. These two bands should never meet.

Now we move from heroes to villains. Morrissey opened his 2004 tour dates with Pete Wylie's 'Imperfect List', on which Josie Jones reads an inventory of pet hates in a caustic scouse accent: 'Adolf Hitler, Mike Gatting, Terry and June, fucking bastard Thatcher . . .' Call it 'Reasons to be Fearful', or 'My Least Favourite Things'.

Johnny Cash's breakneck travelogue 'I've Been Everywhere' is good stuff but he never crosses the Atlantic. For a better approximation of 'everywhere', try Lemon Jelly's exquisite 'Ramblin' Man'. Actor John Standing rolls the name of each exotic locale around his mouth like it's a Werther's Original. More *joie de vivre* from Nina Simone, who ticks off what she hasn't got (money, family, God) and then what she has (hair, liver, etc.), all with no-time-to-waste gusto.

The last two songs rely on sheer verbal volume. Antonio Carlos Jobim's classic 'Águas de Março' is an impressionistic torrent of nouns representing the journey of life towards death (in Brazil, March rains mark the end of summer). REM's own word splurge was inspired, obliquely, by the rise of twenty-four-hour news. It suggests two voices in the same head, Michael Stipe mimicking the frantic burble of data overload ('Uh-oh, overflow!'), while Mike Mills pleads for quiet ('Time I spent some time alone'). It's the sound of list fatigue.

THE PLAYLIST

The Intro and the Outro The Bonzo Dog Band

Feel Good Hit of the Summer Queens of the Stone Age

People Who Died Jim Carroll

Hot Topic Le Tigre

Can U Dig It? Pop Will Eat Itself

Imperfect List (Mix 2) Big Hard Excellent Fish

Ramblin' Man Lemon Jelly

Ain't Got No – I Got Life Nina Simone

Águas de Março (Waters of March) Antonio Carlos Jobim and
  Elis Regina

It's the End of the World As We Know It (And I Feel Fine)
  REM

CRIME

(▶) Weighing up the candidates for this playlist was the musical equivalent of watching nothing but *CSI* for a week: a bloodbath with a beat. I sat through numberless tales of drug dealing, rape and, especially, homicide, from your common-or-garden shootings and stabbings to more outré methods of dispatch such as driving your pregnant girlfriend off a bridge (Eminem's Stan) or swinging a silver hammer (the Beatles' Maxwell).

But we begin on an atypically upbeat note. Songs about getting busted don't come more exuberant than the Crickets' 'I Fought the Law', especially when it's performed by the Clash. The Killers live up to their name on 'Jenny Was a Friend of Mine', a murderous boyfriend's confession made thoroughly credible by Brandon Flowers's creepy, stop-me-before-I-kill-again real-life demeanour. I could happily have filled this playlist with hip-hop but for sheer malevolence it's hard to beat 'Natural Born Killaz', a lurid psychodrama ('I don't understand the logic in my dreams / But I understand I like the sound of sirens') set to nightmarish gothic funk.

Black America's most enduring murder narrative is the tale of Stagolee. The story, like the spelling, changes depending on the singer, stretching from Cab Calloway to Nick Cave. In Mississippi John

Hurt's riveting 1928 interpretation, Stagolee's a cold-blooded bastard who kills a man for a five-dollar stetson: the original gangsta. The Stagolee myth stemmed from a real murder in St Louis in 1895; the kidnap and rape of a fourteen-year-old girl in Tacoma, Washington almost a hundred years later inspired Nirvana's chilling 'Polly', sung from the rapist's perspective. After that, some petty crime comes as a relief. It could have been Supergrass's 'Caught by the Fuzz' or Ian Dury's 'Razzle in My Pocket' but let's have the Slits' punchy ode to the five-finger discount. Ari Up squawks us through the economics: 'Ten quid for the lot. We pay *fack all*!'

Cinema inspired the next two songs. From the soundtrack to landmark Jamaican gangster film *The Harder They Come*, the Slickers' 'Johnny Too Bad' simultaneously berates and mythologises a knife-wielding rude boy. Serge Gainsbourg cashed in on the zeitgeisty success of Arthur Penn's *Bonnie and Clyde* (or, as Serge would have it, *Burny and Clyyyde*) via this mellifluous duet with lover Brigitte Bardot. He wrote it in a single night as penance after a disastrous date.

Canadian three-hit wonder R. Dean Taylor must have been immersed in crime movies when he wrote 'Indiana Wants Me' in the form of a fugitive's letter to his girlfriend and baby. With sirens at the beginning and police megaphones at the end ('You are surrounded, give yourself up'), it's a cornball masterpiece. I'm fast coming to the conclusion that everything sounds better sung by Ella Fitzgerald, so it has to be her version of 'Miss Otis Regrets (She's Unable to Lunch

Today)', Cole Porter's song about a woman who misses a lunch date on account of being hanged for shooting her lover. As excuses go, it's hard to argue with.

THE PLAYLIST

I Fought the Law   The Clash
Jenny Was a Friend of Mine   The Killers
Natural Born Killaz   Ice Cube and Dr Dre
Stack o' Lee Blues   Mississippi John Hurt
Polly   Nirvana
Shoplifting   The Slits
Johnny Too Bad   The Slickers
Bonnie and Clyde   Serge Gainsbourg and Brigitte Bardot
Indiana Wants Me   R. Dean Taylor
Miss Otis Regrets (She's Unable to Lunch Today)
   (1956 version)   Ella Fitzgerald

CARS AND DRIVING

(▶) Something about this topic makes me feel suddenly very British. In American rock, the automobile and the open road are clichés worn to a nub by the likes of Bruce Springsteen, with his gusty melodramas about young guns escaping two-bit towns on wheels of faith down highways of glory, and so on. Give me the deadpan wit and Ballardian psychodrama of British road songs any day.

Inside every driver lurks a miniature Jeremy Clarkson, and Golden Earring's irresistible paean to the long-distance booty call will bring him frothing to the surface, banging on about horsepower and the Germans. Speaking of whom, Kraftwerk's Ralf Hütter has explained of his group's twenty-two-minute masterpiece 'Autobahn', 'the cars hum a melody'. Indeed, it's a driving song which seems to eliminate the human driver. The refrain of 'wir fahren fahren fahren' echoes the Beach Boys' 'Fun Fun Fun', replacing teenage heat with the dispassionate cool of machines on the move.

Rock 'n' roll and the automobile, those twin emblems of freedom for American teens, were intertwined from the get-go. The Ike Turner-penned 1951 single often regarded as the first ever rock 'n' roll record celebrates the Oldsmobile 88. Metaphor-lovers, however, will quickly ascertain that the real object of Jackie Brenston's enthusiasm is his penis. Prince's first big hit takes automotive innuendo as far as it will go before turning into *Carry On Up the Exhaust Pipe*.

In songs such as Junior Walker's '(I'm a) Road Runner', the dust is never allowed to settle. Lucinda Williams articulates the downside of a tumbleweed existence with this autobiographical, child's-eye perspective of a life in constant flux. The five-year-old Lucinda is the reluctant passenger watching 'telephone poles, trees and wires fly by' from the back seat while her parents make plans in the front. Stiff Records producer Larry Wallis's playfully menacing 'Police Car' is one of the only songs written from a vehicle's point of view.

J.G. Ballard's *Crash* birthed a new kind of driving song, one that saw cars as agents of alienation, destruction or erotic collision. It explicitly inspired 'Warm Leatherette' by Mute Records founder Daniel Miller. Over the squeal and hiss of machines in torment, Miller steers the car/sex relationship to places Jackie Brenston never imagined: 'A tear of petrol is in your eye / The handbrake penetrates your thigh.' For Bowie in the enthralling 'Always Crashing in the Same Car', collision isn't a thrill but the symbol of a life going nowhere: he's born not to run.

There is something undeniably feeble about Britain's clotted arteries contrasted with America's endless spacious highways. Billy Bragg milked it for every drop of bathos when he rewrote 'Route 66' as 'A13, Trunk Road to the Sea' ('If you ever go to Shoeburyness . . .') but it's much harder, surely, to grant some measure of romance to

those mundane As and Ms. To deliciously perverse pop trio Black Box
Recorder, 'the English motorway system is beautiful and strange', and
It's Immaterial hit the M62 with a nocturnal travelogue that makes
northern England every bit as worthy of musical celebration as
Barstow or San Bernardino.

THE PLAYLIST

Radar Love Golden Earring
Autobahn Kraftwerk
Rocket 88 Jackie Brenston and his Delta Cats
Little Red Corvette Prince
Car Wheels on a Gravel Road Lucinda Williams
Police Car Larry Wallis
Warm Leatherette The Normal
Always Crashing in the Same Car David Bowie
The English Motorway System Black Box Recorder
Driving Away From Home (Jim's Tune) It's Immaterial

MAMMALS

▶ Most songs nominally about mammals are nothing of the sort. Al Stewart's 'Year of the Cat' is conspicuously pussless and Black Sabbath's 'War Pigs' contains no more pork than a Jewish cookbook. Conversely, the more literal the animal reference, the rummer the song. The Shaggs' heartfelt plea to their lost dog, 'My Pal Foot Foot', is so unwittingly disturbing that it will haunt your dreams, and Michael Jackson's 'Ben' is a famously embarrassing ode to a pet rat, although if Jackson had continued to confine his affections to rodents then his life would have been significantly less complicated.

Between the irrelevant and the bizarre lurk a few artists who are genuinely obsessed with the animal world (the Cure) and many more who are suckers for an easy metaphor. Horses signify romance and adventure, rats treachery, and poor old pigs pretty much every vice you can imagine.

Is there a record more ferally exciting than the Stooges' 'I Wanna Be Your Dog'? From Iggy's hair-raising yelp of 'Come on!' to that strangled howl of a guitar solo, it sounds as if it's about to pounce, slavering, from the speakers. The Cramps cross-bred the Stooges' bestial sexuality with the innocent dance-craze R'n'B of Rufus Thomas's 'Can Your Monkey Do the Dog' to create a mischievous pop mongrel.

Syd Barrett's 'Lucifer Sam' is either about his girlfriend Jennifer Spires, an evil spirit or a bona fide Siamese cat. Either way, it's rollicking garage-rock, one of the few instances in which Barrett's frazzled whimsy grows teeth. Julian Cope's psychedelic three-parter 'Reynard the Fox' – English folklore by way of the Doors – takes the side of a breathless, bloodied fox fleeing a pack of hunters.

Before his Amarillo-sized comeback, crooner Tony Christie enjoyed an unlikely mini-revival as the cuckolded lover clinging on to his pride in the All Seeing I's wonderful, Jarvis Cocker-penned 1999 hit 'Walk Like a Panther'. I bet Cocker's a fan of puckish French songwriter Georges Brassens, who incurred the disapproval of French radio in 1952 with 'Le Gorille', the tale of a well-endowed ape sodomising a ruthless judge. Jake Thackray recorded a very funny English translation.

There's sex of a more conventional variety in 'Pony'. 'Ride it, my pony,' invites R'n'B rake Ginuwine. 'My saddle's waiting / Come and jump on it.' You get the gist. Timbaland's distinctive bassline, seemingly supplied by belching robots, still sounds fresh a decade later. There's room for one more horse song: Jagger and Richards's magnificently weary 'Wild Horses', caked in prairie dust by Gram Parsons' Flying Burrito Brothers.

Wild animals are often idealised as an antidote to human failings. In the Pixies' 'Caribou', named after the north American reindeer, Black Francis complains 'I live cement' and dreams of 'wide ground to run'. There's a similar desire to escape civilisation in Fred Neil's hippie-folk standard 'Dolphins', which Tim Buckley performs with his usual quivering intensity. A wonderful song, but I find the message too sentimental. I prefer the paranoid muttering of the Talking Heads' 'Animals': 'I know the animals are laughing at us.'

THE PLAYLIST

I Wanna Be Your Dog The Stooges
Can Your Pussy Do the Dog? The Cramps
Lucifer Sam Pink Floyd
Reynard the Fox Julian Cope
Walk Like a Panther The All Seeing I
Le Gorille Georges Brassens
Pony Ginuwine
Wild Horses The Flying Burrito Brothers
Caribou Pixies
Dolphins Tim Buckley

THE SUPERNATURAL

(▶) Songwriters venture into the realm of ghosts and ghouls at their peril. You try to explore the inky catacombs of the paranormal and you end up evoking a coven of chalk-faced teenagers drinking cider beneath a small-town war memorial. In fact, many of the records which provoke a shudder of horror down your spine and a hot bubble of nausea in your stomach have nothing to do with the supernatural – Duran Duran's covers album, for example.

On to the good stuff. 'I Put a Spell on You' was the outlandish signature tune of rock 'n' roll eccentric Screamin' Jay Hawkins. Several artists, including Nina Simone, have reinterpreted this voodoo love song but none have emulated the eldritch magic of Hawkins's cackling, unhinged performance, fuelled by a considerable amount of scotch. Proto-goths the Cramps made a career out of fusing primitive rockabilly, punk spirit and monster-movie schlock. 'Human Fly', with its malevolent, buzzing vocal, kicked it all off.

Horror movies are so much a part of our cultural vocabulary that smart songwriters can have fun with them. The undead narrator of 'I'm a Vampire' by Stephin Merritt's synth-pop side-project Future Bible Heroes explains the advantages of a blood-sucking existence with villainous relish: 'Survived for seven hundred years and still look seventeen.' On the viciously funny 'Werewolves of London', Warren Zevon tells of a 'hairy-handed gent who ran amok in Kent'. *A-hoooo*!

Not just caucasian but Canadian, R. Dean Taylor seemed to owe his place on the 1960s Motown roster to a clerical error. Nevertheless, he recorded a couple of imperishable classics, including this northern soul foot-stomper about a man tormented by the memory of his former girlfriend. Kristin Hersh takes the same conceit as R. Dean Taylor and imbues it with a lilting intimacy. Michael Stipe shadows her on the chorus like the absent (dead?) ex-lover to whom the song is addressed.

Two arrestingly strange top twenty hits next. Synthesisers whisper and mutter like digital phantoms on Japan's desolate ballad 'Ghosts'. Remarkable to think that it reached number five in 1981. A Guy Called Gerald used to claim that 1989's 'Voodoo Ray' was cursed because his career was subsequently plagued by thieving managers and collapsing record labels. The idea doesn't sound too far-fetched when you revisit its flickering, half-lit groove and shamanic vocal: house music as eerie ritual. 'I had this idea of people locking into a beat, this picture of a voodoo ceremony,' Gerald later explained.

Listening to Dr John's 'I Walk on Guilded Splinters', you'd think the real thing was taking place in the studio; as the New Orleans legend inhabits the persona of a murderous medicine man, you can picture chickens having their throats cut over the mixing desk. Finally, Jerry Dammers wrote 'Ghost Town' after witnessing grim visions of urban decay while on tour in Glasgow, and then watched it soundtrack the riots that shook Britain during the summer of 1981. The title's a figure of speech, of course, but the distant police sirens, wailing like wraiths, make it sound like the real thing.

THE PLAYLIST

I Put a Spell on You Screamin' Jay Hawkins
Human Fly The Cramps
I'm a Vampire Future Bible Heroes
Werewolves of London Warren Zevon
There's a Ghost in My House R. Dean Taylor
Your Ghost Kristin Hersh
Ghosts Japan
Voodoo Ray A Guy Called Gerald
I Walk on Guilded Splinters Dr John
Ghost Town The Specials

FRIENDSHIP

(▶) Given that so many sitcom theme tunes celebrate friendship, it's no wonder that many songs celebrating friendship resemble sitcom theme tunes – except the really earnest ones, like Coldplay's 'Fix You', which would be better suited to soundtracking a poignant montage in a *Holby City* Christmas special. The flaw in such big comfort-rock pick-me-ups, stretching from 'Fix You' back to 'You've Got a Friend', is their fuzzy, undiscriminating embrace. They capture none of the grit and grain of real friendships. I'd rather have the chatty intimacy of Michelle Shocked's 'Anchorage' or the woozy ambiguity of the Lemonheads' 'My Drug Buddy'.

Jerry Seinfeld used to have a good routine about the easy logic of childhood friendships: 'You like candy? I like candy! Let's be friends!' That uncomplicated bonding is the theme of the White Stripes' gentlest song, one so expertly crafted that it makes me feel nostalgic for someone else's youth. A playground mentality also informed the Spice Girls' 'Wannabe', back when they really were friends and not a tense coalition of dysfunctional celebrities. Looking back, it sounds surprisingly, klutzily innocent.

Not all companionship is welcome. Justice vs Simian's 'We Are Your Friends', one of the decade's most tenacious dance records, rams home its claim with such manic, stalkerish intensity that you wonder: do you really want them to be your friends? In 'Are "Friends" Electric?', Gary Numan threads genuine feelings of alienation (he is mildly autistic) and Philip K. Dick's sci-fi fantasias into the story of a man whose robot buddy has broken down.

By contrast, the friendship in Dinosaur Jr's proto-grunge classic 'Freak Scene' is all too messily human. It's a tender, ragged anthem for mutually dependent screw-ups everywhere: 'Don't let me fuck up will you / Cuz when I need a friend it's still you / What a mess.' Willie Nelson's 'Me and Paul' has its own brand of scuffed-up honesty, fondly and wittily commemorating a bond (with drummer Paul English) forged on the road: 'Almost busted in Laredo / But for reasons that I'd rather not disclose.'

In the Clash's wonderful, underrated 'Stay Free', Mick Jones addresses two estranged schoolmates fresh out of prison. Life sort of imitated art over twenty years later, when Jones produced the second Libertines album after Pete Doherty had served time for burgling the flat of bandmate Carl Barât. Along with 'What Became of the Likely Lads', 'Can't Stand Me Now' vividly describes – indeed acts out – a friendship in terminal decline.

Bonnie 'Prince' Billy's 'I See a Darkness' is comfort-rock's negative image. Here, the narrator's friend doesn't just offer a sympathetic ear after a hard day at work, but deliverance from the shadowy corners of his soul. Johnny Cash's cracked-earth croak makes those shadowy corners frighteningly credible. Oh, all right, let's end on a bona fide heart-warmer. To my ears, 'Lean on Me' transcends corniness to become a kind of secular hymn – one with a much lighter touch than, say, 'Bridge Over Troubled Water'. I suspect that this is the song Chris Martin most wishes he'd written. Either this or the theme from *Cheers*.

THE PLAYLIST

We're Going to Be Friends   The White Stripes
Wannabe   The Spice Girls
We Are Your Friends   Justice vs Simian
Are 'Friends' Electric?   Tubeway Army
Freak Scene   Dinosaur Jr
Me and Paul   Willie Nelson
Stay Free   The Clash
Can't Stand Me Now   The Libertines
I See a Darkness   Johnny Cash
Lean on Me   Bill Withers

GUNS

(▶) In the summer of 2006, Tory leader David Cameron continued an ignoble political tradition of scapegoating trigger-happy rap lyrics. His shallow opportunism was no great surprise, but some of his critics were equally simplistic in their defence of hip-hop, applying the say-what-you-see defence to lyrics that are no more sincere reportage than *Scarface* is a poignant meditation on the plight of Cuban immigrants.

The point is not that rappers don't revel in the drama of flying bullets: it's that they're not alone. Guns have always been a guilty pleasure for storytellers. In American music you can trace the tradition back through Johnny Cash shooting a man in Reno just to watch him die and Robert Johnson cradling his 32-20 rifle to the legend of Stagolee, the mythology of the old west and the Second Amendment.

Even socially conscious songwriters romanticise the gun if they consider the cause righteous. Alabama 3 based 'Woke Up This Morning' on the true story of a woman who shot dead her abusive husband, not that you can hear it now without picturing Tony Soprano's long drive home. 'Hey Joe' has the dark resonance of a folk tale. It's been passed on like a folk tale, too, with versions by Love, Deep Purple, Ice-T and Cher, among others, but Hendrix owns it with his ominous, uncoiling machismo.

The gun is also a – ahem – loaded political metaphor. In Magazine's thrillingly tense post-punk landmark 'Shot by Both Sides', Howard Devoto portrays himself as a lone dissenter caught in the era's ideological crossfire. To the perpetually peeved Rage Against the Machine, the bullet represents government propaganda. The lyrics may be as subtle as, well, a bullet in the head but such explosive, escalating ire doesn't really call for subtlety.

In the anti-gun camp, Gang of Four take aim at the emblematic firearm of the Ulster conflict, the Armalite, and the Valentines tackle the epidemic of gun violence in 1960s Jamaica, albeit in such a chirpy manner that you'd think they were all for it. Lynyrd Skynyrd contradict their good-ol'-boy image with 'Saturday Night Special', a thunderous, NRA-bothering demand for gun control, and Steve Earle offers a rollicking morality tale in which, contrary to his mama's warnings, our pistol-packing hero shoots dead a card cheat. Doesn't he know that characters in country songs should always heed their mama?

Hip-hop has more to say about guns and their uses than any other genre, and I've never encountered a more eloquent and original example than 'I Gave You Power'. Nas, a fascinatingly conflicted MC with a compassionate angel on one shoulder and a gangsta devil on the other, imagines himself as a gun that's finally grown sick of killing: 'I might have took your first child / Scarred your life, crippled your style / I gave you power.' The narrative grips like a fist. We end not with a whimper but a 'Bang Bang': written for Cher, turned inside out by Nancy Sinatra and Lee Hazlewood and made shockingly literal by Quentin Tarantino in *Kill Bill*.

THE PLAYLIST

Woke Up This Morning (Chosen One mix) Alabama 3
Hey Joe Jimi Hendrix
Shot by Both Sides Magazine
Bullet in the Head Rage Against the Machine
Armalite Rifle Gang of Four
Blam Blam Fever The Valentines
Saturday Night Special Lynyrd Skynyrd
The Devil's Right Hand Steve Earle
I Gave You Power Nas
Bang Bang (My Baby Shot Me Down) Nancy Sinatra

SELF-REFERENTIAL
SONGS

(▶) Most pop aspires to suspend disbelief. Even autobiographical songwriters rarely address the camera, so to speak, and declare that it's all just showbiz. Indeed it would be very trying if everybody did. In a decade apparently hellbent on demystifying pop, Eminem and Robbie Williams provide running commentaries on their own careers, but that requires keen self-knowledge and a good sense of humour. Deliver us from witless solipsists who expose nothing but their own hollowness.

Some examples are confusing. My Robot Friend wrote 'We're the Pet Shop Boys' as homage, only for the Pet Shop Boys to record it themselves, and Sparks covered 'We Are the Clash', despite being patently not the Clash. Reassuringly, the Monkees (hey hey) really were the Monkees.

Self-referential pop flirts with smugness but I reckon the sheer art-punk exuberance of Art Brut's 'Formed a Band' mitigates the smart-aleckry. It's a perfect statement of intent, as is 'Antmusic', in which Adam seizes his early 1980s pop crown by decreeing that all music not made by himself is rubbish.

Artists with established reputations can play games with them. In 1978 John Lydon built a funeral pyre for his Johnny Rotten persona and called it Public Image Ltd. In this song's fierce, cleansing rush, he savages clueless fans ('You never listened to a word I said / You only seen me for the clothes I wear') and signs off – rather wonderfully for a debut single – with the word 'goodbye'. On 'Glass Onion', John Lennon mocks his own followers with a string of allusions to past hits and Paul-is-dead rumours, attempting to puncture the Beatles myth from within.

Long before hip-hop there was Bo Diddley, the cocky, self-aggrandising rock 'n' roll forefather who namechecked himself in countless songs, this one being the first and best. After his transition from Massive Attack sidekick to glowering solo star, Tricky twisted rap's tradition of self-promotion into a dense tangle of muttered threats, religious imagery and caustically ambivalent reflections on fame: 'Everybody wants to be naked and famous / Everybody wants to be just like me.'

Touring is a drag, but not as much as songs about touring being a drag. So what makes 'Range Life' different? Maybe the laconic humour, the wistful air, the absence of self-pity and the irreverent references to touring partners Smashing Pumpkins (who were, amusingly, less than pleased). The Arctic Monkeys spent most of their first year in the public eye seeming faintly aggrieved by their own success. On this compellingly conflicted EP track, Alex Turner is by turns neurotic and defiant: 'Bring on the backlash!'

From the micro-genre of history-of-the-band songs I've picked two. Washington DC indie heroes the Minutemen inspired a documentary (*We Jam Econo*) and a book (*Our Band Could Be Your Life*) but they told their own story first, and in just 132 seconds. Mott the Hoople's Ian Hunter wrote pop's most autobiographical farewell single, a three-hankie retrospective culminating in a massed chorus of 'Goodbye'. Sorry, I appear to have something in my eye.

THE PLAYLIST

Formed a Band Art Brut
Antmusic Adam and the Ants
Public Image Public Image Ltd.
Glass Onion The Beatles
Bo Diddley Bo Diddley
Tricky Kid Tricky
Range Life Pavement
Who the Fuck Are Arctic Monkeys? Arctic Monkeys
History Lesson Pt 2 The Minutemen
Saturday Gigs (alternate version) Mott the Hoople

DUETS

(▶) I blame Natalie Cole. When she resurrected her dear dead dad for one last performance on 1991's 'Unforgettable', she changed the duet for ever. No longer would a condition as insignificant as not breathing restrict a singer's availability. 2005's Notorious BIG album *Duets* could scarcely have been less dignified had they exhumed the rapper's skeleton and wheeled it down the street trailing a promotional banner.

To call the modern duet a shotgun wedding would imply too much romance. It's more like a brand merger. Some vocal partners don't even realise what the other one is singing. On 'Crazy in Love', wonderful though it is, Beyoncé and Jay-Z are head over heels for the same person: Jay-Z. So I've confined this list to duets with a strong dynamic, performed by two living people, preferably in the same studio. I've also had to sacrifice a few classics (Peter Gabriel and Kate Bush, Pet Shop Boys and Dusty) to keep things interesting.

Who'd have thought that Cole Porter's droll double-header from *High Society* would fare so well in the hands of two punk icons? Iggy and Debbie don't just enjoy themselves more than Bing and Frank; they have better comic timing. Sliding a few rungs down the social ladder, Otis Redding and Carla Thomas make bickering fun.

Until Tammi Terrell's death from a brain tumour in 1970, she and

Marvin Gaye were Motown's perfect pairing. Their own 'You're All I Need to Get By' is sublime but so is Method Man and Mary J. Blige's remake. In this early example of the so-called 'thug-love duet', the gruff rapper demonstrates that chivalry is not dead, just very, very stoned. Let's take a break from boy-girl duets with Freddie Mercury and David Bowie's fretful melodrama 'Under Pressure', although the real scene-stealer is John Deacon's bassline.

Country music is the spiritual home of the duet: Johnny and June, George and Tammy, Kenny and Dolly. Bobbie Gentry and Glen Campbell made one album together in 1968, featuring this warm breeze of a love song. Lee Hazlewood and Nancy Sinatra founded the gravel-and-honey school of duetting. 'Some Velvet Morning' is magnificently strange and haunting, changing gear with each vocal shift, as if two completely different songs had been spliced together.

Of the latter-day Nancy and Lees, I've chosen Mazzy Star's Hope Sandoval and the Jesus and Mary Chain's Jim Reid. 'Sometimes Always' is simply perfect: a break-up, a reunion and genuine chemistry between the leads, even though Sandoval was actually dating Reid's brother William. A long way from the country tradition, Björk and Thom Yorke's eerie industrial show tune is the only good thing about *Dancer in the Dark*, a film so grotesquely mawkish that I actually cheered up when Björk's character was executed.

Finally, two premature festive pairings. Louis Jordan uses inclement weather as a ploy to get Ella Fitzgerald into bed, while

Shane MacGowan and Kirsty MacColl scrap on the streets of Manhattan, striking a flawless balance between grit and sentimentality.

THE PLAYLIST

Well Did You Evah! Iggy Pop and Deborah Harry
Tramp Otis Redding (with Carla Thomas)
I'll Be There for You / You're All I Need to Get By
   (Puff Daddy mix) Method Man (with Mary J. Blige)
Under Pressure Queen and David Bowie
Mornin' Glory Bobbie Gentry and Glen Campbell
Some Velvet Morning Lee Hazlewood and Nancy Sinatra
Sometimes Always The Jesus and Mary Chain
   (with Hope Sandoval)
I've Seen It All Björk (with Thom Yorke)
Baby It's Cold Outside Ella Fitzgerald and Louis Jordan
Fairytale of New York The Pogues (with Kirsty MacColl)

VISUAL ART

(▶) Irritating people like to recite Frank Zappa's (or possibly Elvis Costello's) legendary non-witticism to the effect that writing about music is like dancing about architecture, despite its being neither funny nor true. But what about singing about visual art? Even with art schools' noble history of nurturing pop talent, from John Lennon to Franz Ferdinand, the subject rarely makes it into song. The Rolling Stones' 'Paint It, Black' is really more concerned with decorating.

So references tend to be fleeting. There's Jarvis Cocker's tryst with a sculpture student in 'Common People'; Joni Mitchell's jazz club dauber in 'The Jungle Line'; the Manic Street Preachers' nods to Picasso and de Kooning; and the poor girl in the Stone Roses' 'Going Down', who 'looks like a painting: Jackson Pollock's *Number Five*'. For brevity and accuracy, you can't beat Ian Dury's 'There Ain't Half Been Some Clever Bastards' (which, incidentally, would make an excellent new title for Radio 4's *In Our Time*). Of Van Gogh, Dury rightly notes: 'He didn't do the *Mona Lisa* / That was an Italian geezer.'

Let's start with King Missile's very funny takedown of an artist so sensitive that he can't even attend galleries, 'because there are people there / And I can't deal with people.' You know the type. The waggish Art Brut snub elitism by making Hockney and Matisse sound as fun as the Stooges and the Clash: 'Modern art makes me want to rock out!' But modern art is bad news for the hero of the Creation's 'Painter Man', a 1960s art school graduate who finds that 'classic art has had its day' and ends up illustrating food labels.

The Rezillos' effervescent art-school romance takes us to five songs about five artists, starting with the *Mona Lisa*, famously painted by an Italian geezer (thanks, Ian) and later pondered by Nat King Cole. But Cole wasn't much of an art critic, unlike prog-rock highbrows King Crimson, who elaborate the story behind Rembrandt's *The Night Watch* with the gusto of gallery tour guides. For trendy 1970s art teachers this must have been manna from heaven.

L.S. Lowry has inspired two songs. Brian and Michael's 'Matchstalk Men and Matchstalk Cats and Dogs' is too twee for any-one over the age of ten, but suspend any anti-Quo prejudices you may have because 'Pictures of Matchstick Men' is a stand-alone psychedelic classic. When Andy Warhol died, Lou Reed and John Cale stopped hating each other long enough to record a whole album dedicated to their late benefactor, *Songs for Drella*. Cale channels Warhol on 'Trouble with Classicists', a wonderfully dry iconoclast's manifesto.

The Brit-art glitterati haven't been as fondly regarded. 'Private View (I'm Not Going to Your Boring)' is good fly-in-the-ointment stuff from Billy Childish's Buff Medways but I'll go with Luke Haines's comically intemperate fantasies about Sarah Lucas. Felt's career – ten albums in ten years – had the conceptual purity of an art project.

'Primitive Painters' bemoans, with great charm, extravagant beauty and a goosebump-raising cameo from Liz Fraser, the plight of the sensitive artist. And that's where we came in.

THE PLAYLIST

Sensitive Artist King Missile
Modern Art Art Brut
Painter Man The Creation
(My Baby Does) Good Sculptures The Rezillos
Mona Lisa Nat King Cole
The Night Watch King Crimson
Pictures of Matchstick Men Status Quo
Trouble with Classicists Lou Reed and John Cale
Death of Sarah Lucas Luke Haines
Primitive Painters Felt

COCAINE AND HEROIN

▶ Reading suggestions for this playlist, I began to feel like Robert De Niro in *Meet the Parents* when he's informed of 'Puff the Magic Dragon's alleged hidden meaning and huffily retorts, 'Puff is just the name of the boy's magical dragon.' I may be naïve but I'm pretty sure that 'The Drugs Don't Work' describes hospital treatment, 'Eight Miles High' deals with air travel and the title of Nick Cave's 'Into My Arms' does not refer to hypodermics. Even with Lou Reed's 'Perfect Day', the narcotic subtext of which has often been rumoured but never confirmed, I wonder why the man who once called a song 'Heroin' would suddenly become so coy. And is the zoo really such a big junkie hotspot?

Anyway, J.J. Cale's tense blues rumble 'Cocaine' is the Ronseal of drug songs. Unless, of course, he's using cocaine as a euphemism for sugar or snow, but that seems unlikely. 'Prangin' Out' was already an unsettling depiction of snowbound paranoia before Mike Skinner invited Britain's favourite drug addict to add a grimly candid guest verse. 'Prang's a night that gets darker and darker,' slurs Pete Doherty, like a man a long way from dawn.

Hip-hop is tirelessly eloquent on the entrepreneurish aspects of selling crack cocaine – that's how Jay-Z started out – but trust Public

Enemy to count the social cost on the most thrilling just-say-no missive this side of 'White Lines'. James Brown sounds more like Gil Scott-Heron than his funky self on the magnificent spoken-word track 'King Heroin'. A shame the Godfather of Soul wasn't quite so clever on the subject of angel dust. And guns. And leading the police on an interstate car chase.

Dee Dee Ramone wrote 'Chinese Rocks' about Heartbreaker Jerry Nolan. After Tommy Ramone vetoed it, he passed it on to Nolan's bandmates. The lyrics say (I'm paraphrasing here): 'My life is a squalid mess with no hope of improvement.' The music says: 'Let's party!' No ambivalence on 'Golden Brown', a dreamy love song to heroin superficially directed at a well-tanned woman, while the Gun Club reverse the analogy on their mad-eyed ode to a girl who 'cannot miss a vein'.

During the mid-1990s, it seemed quicker to count the American musicians who *weren't* injecting heroin. Whole pages of grunge's songbook are stained brown. I've chosen Elliott Smith's 'Needle in the Hay' because it's so fragile, so broken up inside, and, in its final line ('You ought to be proud that I'm getting good marks'), so shockingly flippant. In the 1970s, Neil Young wrote a clutch of songs about the drug that destroyed Crazy Horse guitarist Danny Whitten. This one is famous for good reason. He's not tubthumping, just softly mourning a friend.

Finally, 'Cop Shoot Cop' is an epic collision of Spiritualized's favourite subjects – heartbreak, heresy and heroin – loosely based on

John Prine's Vietnam-era junk fable 'Sam Stone' and underpinned by the voodoo piano of former addict Dr John: a smack-rock triple word score. But Puff really *is* just a magical dragon.

THE PLAYLIST

Cocaine J.J. Cale

Prangin' Out (Pete and Mike's version) The Streets

Night of the Living Baseheads Public Enemy

King Heroin James Brown

Chinese Rocks Johnny Thunders and the Heartbreakers

Golden Brown The Stranglers

She's Like Heroin to Me The Gun Club

Needle in the Hay Elliott Smith

The Needle and the Damage Done Neil Young

Cop Shoot Cop Spiritualized

FUNNY
SONGS

(▶) Other people's sense of humour is a mysterious thing. If you were to draw a Venn diagram of funny songs, the overlap between one person's idea of comedic nirvana and another's definition of musical hell would be considerable. Generally, I like either tomb-dry one-liners (Leonard Cohen), cheerful idiocy (Sir Mix-A-Lot) or unintentional hilarity (the Doors), and consider the work of Frank Zappa a black hole from which no mirth can escape. But that's just me.

Even the good stuff works best in small doses. Better to write the occasional witty couplet, like Morrissey or Stephin Merritt, than build your whole shtick on a gag. As Goldie Lookin' Chain and the Darkness will dolefully testify, God help you when the laughter dies down. Anyway, these ten songs all made me chuckle at least once. I can't guarantee they'll do the same for everybody.

I tried to exclude all professional comedians from the playlist, but had to make an exception for Spinal Tap's twisted homage to the heroic stupidity of heavy metal. I'm sure there are people who don't find 'Stonehenge' funny but I have no wish to meet them. A list without scouse humourists Half Man Half Biscuit would be no list at all. In 'Breaking News', Nigel Blackwell reels off a droll list of irritants, including 'a woman who described herself as a little bit Bridget, a little bit Ally, a little bit *Sex in the City*' and 'continuity announcers introducing comedy shows'. There's no arguing with that.

The first law of comedy states that there is nothing funnier than being rude about people. So the Undertones stick it to cousin Kevin and Fats Waller proves to be an ungallant date, but they are sweetness and light compared to Lady Sovereign, who rips into grime one-hit wonder Jentina with such hilarious venom that you have to laugh between gasps.

Hip-hop is so obsessed with winners that self-deprecating rappers get comic mileage out of being losers. While most MCs advertise their romantic prowess, the Pharcyde's amiable 'Oh Shit' relates three disastrous hook-ups, including one where she turns out to be a he. 'Looked at her shoes and her feets was real long,' gulps Fatlip. The Bonzo Dog Band, who updated music hall humour for the age of psychedelia, parodied Raymond Chandler on 'Big Shot': 'She had the hottest hips since Hiroshima.' Impeccable delivery and a great punchline which I won't give away here. Jake Thackray's phrasing could raise a titter reading from the Nasdaq. Like the Kinks' 'Lola' and Tone Loc's 'Funky Cold Medina', 'Sister Josephine' stars a woman who is not all she seems: let's just say her feets was real big.

Lemonhead Evan Dando reveals a flair for comedy on 'The Outdoor Type', which could easily be the theme to a sitcom about a lovable slacker who gets nothing done on account of his phenomenal appetite for heroin. You could call it *Knockin' on Evan's Door*. Finally, Phil Ochs's references to Hubert Humphrey and Medgar Evers may have dated but his barbed observations still draw blood.

THE PLAYLIST

Stonehenge Spinal Tap
Breaking News Half Man Half Biscuit
My Perfect Cousin The Undertones
Your Feet's Too Big Fats Waller
Sad Arse Strippa Lady Sovereign
Oh Shit The Pharcyde
Big Shot The Bonzo Dog Band
Sister Josephine Jake Thackray
The Outdoor Type The Lemonheads
Love Me, I'm a Liberal Phil Ochs

GOING OUT

(▶) The opening lines of the first Arctic Monkeys album take an unromantic view of the great British night out, with Alex Turner singing, 'Anticipation has the habit to set you up / For disappointment in evening entertainment, but . . .' It's that emphatic 'but' on which the album – in fact the whole going-out genre – pivots. Sure, you might end up underwhelmed and under the weather, vomiting through the window of an unlicensed minicab, but . . . you might just have the time of your life. The yin of messy realism ('Friday Night Saturday Morning', 'Bedsitter') needs the yang of soaring optimism ('I Love the Nightlife', 'Off the Wall').

We start with the most unlikely party host. On 'All Tomorrow's Parties', the fathomlessly sombre Nico sounds like some Dickensian ghost haunting the festivities with bad tidings for all. Who better to blast out the cobwebs than Andrew W.K., a man for whom partying demands the same bellicose conviction as a military operation? This gonzo-metal rampage is the *Platoon* of party records. Back in Britain, the Kaiser Chiefs take time out from riot-predicting to have a good time on 'Saturday Night'.

I've never gone to a go-go, or even been to a be-be, but the Miracles make it seem like the alpha and omega of good times. Staying in can be good too, provided you have enough company. Lacking the necessary cab fare and disco duds, James Brown sideman Fred Wesley throws an impromptu bash of his own. 'We might disturb the neighbors but I'll take that chance,' he brags, blissfully unbothered by ASBO-wielding noise abatement officers. The Associates come across like Wesley's nightmare guests on 'Party Fears Two', barging through the door to the sound of a manically perky piano riff and Billy MacKenzie's mad, voluptuous wail. 'Have I done something wrong?' Yes, he probably has.

Things get blurrier still with the anarchic bovver-disco of '24 Hour Party People', sung – or rather 'sung' – by Shaun Ryder in the manner of someone who has consumed all the drugs in Manchester. I like to think that the Happy Mondays' party is the one that an aghast Three Dog Night find themselves trapped in on their version of Randy Newman's wry wallflower's lament 'Mama Told Me Not to Come'. 'That ain't no way to have fun,' they yelp, as Ryder gurningly passes around the temazepam.

Time to rewind to the start of the evening with two songs which tingle with possibility. 'Steppin' Out' floods the prospect of a night in the city with romance and yearning: 'We'll leave the TV and the radio behind / Don't you wonder what we'll find?' Even the cantering bassline seems to be hurrying you out of the door. Some call 'Downtown' corny but I find its vision of a neon utopia, inspired by songwriter Tony Hatch's first walk down Broadway, immensely moving, as if all the troubles in the world can be forgotten in a stroke. Play them both before leaving the house for a night out. Anticipation is a wonderful thing.

THE PLAYLIST

All Tomorrow's Parties The Velvet Underground

Party Hard Andrew W.K.

Saturday Night Kaiser Chiefs

Going to a Go-Go Smokey Robinson and the Miracles

House Party Fred Wesley

Party Fears Two The Associates

24 Hour Party People Happy Mondays

Mama Told Me (Not to Come) Three Dog Night

Steppin' Out Joe Jackson

Downtown Petula Clark

NAMED AFTER DATES

▶ I compiled this playlist in 2007, a year with neither the millennial resonance of 1999 (Prince) and 2000 (Pulp), nor the time-is-now urgency of 1969 (the Stooges) and 1977 (the Clash). This year, the only relevant song is the Fall's 'Acid Priest 2008', but wait a while and you can listen to a passel of tracks about the Mayan doomsday in 2012. Health and the Mayans permitting, some readers might just be around to hear Rush's '2112' in context. But Zager and Evans's hilarious we're-all-doomed prophecy 'In the Year 2525'? Probably not.

Maybe 2007 or 2008 will be celebrated in retrospect, as some as-yet-unknown songwriter's personal milestone, just as with previous 'year' songs: Andrew Eldritch was born in 1959 (Sisters of Mercy), Nicky Wire turned sixteen in 1985 (Manic Street Preachers) and Damon Albarn began dating Justine Frischmann in 1992 (Blur). Or maybe it will have historical significance. Like a singing A.J.P. Taylor, Al Stewart rarely stops flaunting his knowledge of 20th-century events. As for annual dates, the red-letter days fare best: St Swithin's Day (Billy Bragg), Valentine's Day (ABC) and New Year's Day (U2). And let's not forget the 12th of Never.

'Paris 1919' doesn't directly examine the treaty of Versailles – that would be Al's job – but the ghosts of old Europe stalk Cale's crisp orchestration and elliptical lyrics. Meanwhile, New Order's brilliant '1963' prompts thoughts of book depositories and grassy knolls, yet the song is set in January, not November, and the gunman, not the victim, is called Johnny. Go figure.

Loath to squander a *soixante-neuf* pun, Serge Gainsbourg decreed 1969 an *année érotique* on this irresistibly suave duet with Jane Birkin, although I suspect that every *année* was *érotique* for Serge. '1979' is the Smashing Pumpkins' most endearing song, a wistful meditation on impending adulthood – 'a feeling of waiting for something to happen', according to Billy Corgan. London rapper Estelle revisits her hardscrabble childhood in '1980', named after the year 'that God made me'.

Casimir Pulaski was the Polish-born 'father of the American cavalry', remembered by the state of Illinois on the first Monday of every March. (I can't pretend I didn't have to look this up.) In Sufjan Stevens's song, a curiously moving collision of the public and private, it's the day on which his friend (lover?) dies of cancer. For Aimee Mann, Independence Day festivities revive memories of a broken relationship. As she watches the patriotic pyrotechnics overhead, she sighs, magnificently, 'What a waste of gunpowder and sky.'

A concrete title affixed to an abstract piece of music has peculiar power. Talk Talk's gorgeous quasi-pagan hymn 'April 5th' pins the coming of spring to a single day. Dunwich Beach, Autumn, 1960 could be a caption scrawled beneath a faded photograph. When you know that Brian Eno was twelve in 1960, and that Dunwich was near his childhood home in Suffolk, you can read imagined narratives into the eerie stillness and solitude of the music. Finally, Deltron 3030's sci-fi geek-hop masterpiece takes us to the far-flung future. Only 1022 years to go.

THE PLAYLIST

Paris 1919 John Cale

1963 New Order

69 Année Erotique Serge Gainsbourg

1979 Smashing Pumpkins

1980 Estelle

Casimir Pulaski Day Sufjan Stevens

4th of July Aimee Mann

April 5th Talk Talk

Dunwich Beach, Autumn, 1960 Brian Eno

3030 Deltron 3030

CHARACTER
SONGS

(▶) Some storytellers struggle to create a single credible character over the span of a film or novel, so the reduced canvas of a pop song poses a particularly stiff challenge. We remember those few characters that seem to have a life beyond the song: Bowie's tragic cosmonaut Major Tom, or Tom Waits's irascible wanderer Frank.

Ruling out lyrics about real people narrows the field. Stagolee was based on a killer called Lee Sheldon, Mr Bojangles was tap dancer Bill Robinson, Pearl Jam's Jeremy was school shooter Jeremy Wade Delle, and Leonard Cohen's Suzanne was Suzanne Vaillancourt, a friend who really did serve tea with oranges.

Ray Davies was the king of the 1960s character song, from the titular 'Dedicated Follower of Fashion' to the dissolute aristo in 'Sunny Afternoon'. On his envious tribute to school alpha male David Watts, his usual waspishness is softened by real admiration. At the opposite end of the playground hierarchy, Belle and Sebastian's sports-shy toff Lord Anthony receives some blunt advice: 'Shut your mouth, start kicking a football.'

A well-constructed character can be a sleek vehicle for social comment. Whereas most songwriters portrayed 1970s New York as a hellish stinkhole to be escaped at the soonest opportunity, the heroine of Machine's edgy disco classic leaves the Bronx only to be driven off the rails by her overprotective parents. The message? 'Too much love is worse than no love at all.' N*E*R*D channel Curtis Mayfield into a woozy psych-soul sketch of a teenage junkie, while Warren Zevon weaves African wars and Scandinavian mercenaries into a pungent geopolitical ghost story.

Van Morrison always denied 'Madame George' was a drag queen. Lester Bangs, who called the song 'one of the most compassionate pieces of music ever made', begged to differ. Either way, it's an intensely moving meditation on loneliness and belonging, one which conceals as much as it reveals.

Our last four characters are definitely women. Cab Calloway's Minnie, a 'red-hot hoochie coocher' who drifts off into an opium haze, reappeared in songs such as 'Minnie the Moocher's Wedding Day', 'Minnie's a Hepcat Now' and the rarely heard 'Minnie the Moocher and the Spiders from Mars'. When men write about unchaste women, they tend to patronise or pity (why is it Sting's concern whether or not Roxanne puts on the red light? Bugger off, Sting), but there's more pride than shame in Bobbie Gentry's unfeasibly funky tale of a dirt-poor girl who makes her way by sleeping with rich men. It's hard not to cheer when she trumpets, 'You know I mighta been born just plain white trash but Fancy was my name.'

Marianne Faithfull gave Shel Silverstein's song about disappointed housewife Lucy Jordan just the right amount of empathy and ambiguity. Is the happy ending real or just as illusory as Minnie's opium dreams? Finally, the peerless 'Eleanor Rigby': a life – a whole world in fact – in a little over two minutes.

THE PLAYLIST

David Watts The Kinks

Lord Anthony Belle and Sebastian

There but for the Grace of God Go I Machine

Bobby James N*E*R*D

Roland the Headless Thompson Gunner Warren Zevon

Madame George Van Morrison

Minnie the Moocher Cab Calloway

Fancy Bobbie Gentry

The Ballad of Lucy Jordan Marianne Faithfull

Eleanor Rigby The Beatles

MUSICAL GENRES

(▶) It's both funny and revealing that the Killers wrote 'Glamorous Indie Rock & Roll' to poke fun at the snooty, ascetic independent scene in their native Las Vegas, only to find that British audiences, for whom post-Britpop indie is simply pop music with guitars, embraced it as a cheerfully unironic anthem. Useful though they are for those charged with racking or reviewing records, genres are foggy, amorphous things open to countless interpretations. If you want to know the definition of fruitless, just try establishing a watertight distinction between rock and pop.

A song about a genre speaks volumes about the songwriter's agenda. There are tributes to perceived forebears, like Stevie Wonder's 'Sir Duke'; cultural manifestos such as Mos Def's fierce restatement of rock's black roots in 'Rock 'n' Roll'; angry jeremiads, like Nas's 'Hip Hop Is Dead' or Black Rebel Motorcycle Club's 'Whatever Happened to My Rock 'n' Roll'; and, in the case of sitcom actor Paul Nicholas's 'Reggae Like It Used to Be', homages so breathtakingly, unwittingly offensive that they make your head explode.

There's no ignoring our first two songs. In 1979, Malcolm McLaren's art school classmate Robin Scott joined the ranks of one-hit wonders with the wry, puckish 'Pop Muzik', which U2 would later adopt as the theme tune for their PopMart tour. During their formative months in Hamburg, the Beatles attacked Chuck Berry's 'Rock and Roll Music' with such vein-popping ferocity that it seemed to symbolise Britain's imminent hijacking of this American art form.

A special energy is generated when a genre announces its own arrival. In the 1920s, self-appointed 'originator of jazz' Jelly Roll Morton appropriated Joe 'King' Oliver's 'Doctor Jazz' as an ebullient celebration of both the music and his own good self. In 1986, Marshall Jefferson's 'Move Your Body' decreed the house sound of Chicago so new and vital that it made everything else redundant. A generation of clubbers embraced its credo of 'house music all night long'. Reggae was well established by 1976 but, perhaps in retaliation for Paul Nicholas, Bob Marley celebrated it afresh in 'Roots, Rock, Reggae'.

Some genres require justifying. Brooklyn rappers Stetsasonic responded to early criticisms of sampling with 'Talkin' All That Jazz's show-and-tell, backing up its lyrical defence of the sampler's art with an ingenious collage of borrowings from the likes of Lonnie Liston Smith and Donald Byrd. Funkadelic, meanwhile, mocked 1970s genre divisions by asking (and answering) 'Who Says a Funk Band Can't Play Rock?!'

Away from the battle lines, Wilco wistfully recall a long-haired adolescence on 'Heavy Metal Drummer' ('I miss the innocence I've known / Playing Kiss covers, beautiful and stoned'), while Lou Reed's own youthful, epiphanic discovery of rock radio inspires the Velvet

Underground's elevating story of a girl whose 'life was saved by rock 'n' roll'.

Finally, as if in response to all the above, Denim's 'Middle of the Road' dismisses the entire classic-rock canon, moving from the deadpan slaughter of sacred cows towards a stirring call to chart your own path through musical history: a persuasive reminder that genre distinctions are merely a map, not a destination.

THE PLAYLIST

Pop Muzik M

Rock and Roll Music The Beatles

Doctor Jazz Jelly Roll Morton and the Red Hot Peppers

Move Your Body Marshall Jefferson

Roots, Rock, Reggae Bob Marley and the Wailers

Talkin' All That Jazz Stetsasonic

Who Says a Funk Band Can't Play Rock?! Funkadelic

Heavy Metal Drummer Wilco

Rock and Roll The Velvet Underground

Middle of the Road Denim

THE COLD

(▶) When I was a kid, my favourite Christmas carol was 'In the Bleak Midwinter'. Amid the gusty high spirits of 'O Come All Ye Faithful' and the like, Christina Rossetti's words struck a bewitchingly doomy chord. I can't vouch for its historical accuracy, but the stately, doleful repetition had me hooked: 'Snow had fallen / Snow on snow / Snow on snow.' It's the *Velvet Underground and Nico* of carols.

I still think cold weather and music are a good match. When the mercury heads south, some records demand an airing: Joy Division's *Closer*, Radiohead's *Kid A*, Röyksopp's *Melody AM*, some early U2, a lot of Nico, at least three Björk albums, and almost anything by Sigur Rós or Stina Nordenstam (OK, anyone from Iceland). Some evoke the wonder of waking up to a snow-quilted neighbourhood. Others reveal a vast and terrifying Siberia of the soul. You probably don't want to mix them up.

We start with two hard and bitter hearts in need of thawing. The central conceit of Hank Williams's honky-tonk classic 'Cold, Cold Heart' popped up again almost fifty years later in the form of Madonna's billowing techno-goth ballad 'Frozen'. Take your pick.

The Linus Loves remix of 'Ice Skating Girl' is one of the freshest, sweetest dance records of recent years: a New Order sample, an endearingly gawky rap and all the wide-eyed magic of a child's first white Christmas. I defy you not to smile. Barry White could do lavish, uplifting soul as well as anyone, and the title of Love Unlimited Orchestra's Motown-flavoured 'It May Be Winter Outside (But In My Heart It's Spring)' says it all.

Only a band as eccentric and inquiring as British Sea Power could write a song like 'Oh Larsen B'. A love song addressed to a collapsing Antarctic ice shelf, it finds drama in desalination. Similarly unique is 'Pink Frost', the astonishing 1984 single by aptly named New Zealanders the Chills. Narrated by a man cradling a dead lover, its unsettling, otherworldly beauty suggests that it wasn't so much written as summoned from the ether.

Post-punk bands liked their frozen wastelands almost as much as their shadowy underpasses. Magazine's *Secondhand Daylight* album has ice in its veins, and the mesmerising 'Permafrost' ('I will drug you and fuck you on the permafrost') is its numb, sub-zero heart. Meanwhile, the Cure's 'Cold' has a deadly majesty, like an iceberg looming out of the night when it's too late to change course.

The finest track on the Rolling Stones' underrated *Goats Head Soup* album, the epic, yearning ballad 'Winter' is almost a prequel to the Beatles' 'Here Comes the Sun', as if this were the long cold lonely winter George Harrison was singing about. Pretty impressive considering they recorded it in sunny Jamaica. Finally, Galaxie 500 give Yoko Ono's 'Listen, the Snow Is Falling' the space-rock treatment, soft and sparkling at first, then rising to a psychedelic blizzard. I heard this for the first time late one night and woke up to real snow. How perfect is that?

THE PLAYLIST

Cold, Cold Heart Hank Williams

Frozen Madonna

Ice Skating Girl (Linus Loves remix) Rekindle

It May Be Winter Outside (But In My Heart It's Spring) Love Unlimited Orchestra

Oh Larsen B British Sea Power

Pink Frost The Chills

Permafrost Magazine

Cold The Cure

Winter The Rolling Stones

Listen, the Snow Is Falling Galaxie 500

UNREQUITED LOVE

(▶) Thwarted lovers in medieval Europe had the sonnets of Petrarch to echo their pain. Six centuries later, their descendants had David Gedge from the Wedding Present. There will always be a need for art which ennobles an emotion which is, to be honest, a ridiculous waste of time and energy.

Most unrequited love is nothing more than addictive emotional masochism. The more unsuitable or unattainable the object of desire, the stronger the obsession. No wonder even polite young chaps like Chris Martin ('Shiver') and James Blunt (a little song called 'You're Beautiful' – you may have heard it) end up sounding like dangerous loons. Otis Lee Crenshaw's spoof 'Women Call It Stalking' ('She calls it a trial but I call it a date') contains more than a grain of truth. By the way, every song on this playlist was written by a man. Draw your own conclusions.

'I, Who Have Nothing' elevates lovelorn moping to operatic heights. Even the protagonist's fairly pathetic habit of pressing his nose up against the windows of restaurants where his beloved is dining with her fancy-pants boyfriend is rendered heroic. A shame Scott Walker never covered it – that would be the K2 of unrequited love songs – but Ben E. King will do just fine. Coming back down to earth,

Billy Bragg crafts a gently devastating classic about a classroom crush: 'I had to look in the dictionary / To find out the meaning of unrequited.'

There really was a girl from Ipanema, an eighteen-year-old called (deep breath) Heloísa Eneida Menezes Paes Pinto, who used to walk past the Rio bar frequented by songwriters Antonio Carlos Jobim and Vinicius de Moraes. By the end of this sweetly besotted tribute, the listener is hooked too. It flows nicely into the yearning disco of Chic's 'I Want Your Love'.

Mooning over someone else's partner is tricky enough, but some obstacles are even less surmountable. In Fountains of Wayne's power-pop signature tune, a schoolboy lusts over his friend's mum. Going one further, the teenager in 'Pictures of Lily' falls in love with a pin-up who died in 1929, making it the only pop song ever to address the pitfalls of out-of-date erotica.

The Violent Femmes' 'Add It Up' is itchy with pent-up lust. Like an addict, Gordon Gano promises himself 'the day after today I will stop', but the music's rising frenzy suggests otherwise. In 'Auf Achse', named after a 1980s German TV series about truck-drivers, Franz Ferdinand take the tough-love approach towards a lovelorn haulier: 'She's not so special so look what you've done, boy.'

You can't find a more archetypal example of woe-is-me 1980s indie than Another Sunny Day's 99-second mope. Not only does it have the perfect, self-explanatory title, but it manages to make

Morrissey sound like R. Kelly. For our finale, I can understand why Radiohead often seem embarrassed about 'Creep' – it's as painfully transparent as a teenage diary entry – but it's still a masterpiece of poetic self-loathing, every bit as gloriously excessive as 'I, Who Have Nothing'.

THE PLAYLIST

I, Who Have Nothing Ben E. King

The Saturday Boy Billy Bragg

The Girl From Ipanema Astrud Gilberto, Joao Gilberto and
   Stan Getz

I Want Your Love Chic

Stacy's Mom Fountains of Wayne

Pictures of Lily The Who

Add It Up Violent Femmes

Auf Achse Franz Ferdinand

I'm in Love with a Girl who Doesn't Know I Exist
   Another Sunny Day

Creep Radiohead

SONGS ABOUT
THE HEART

▶ On Charlotte 'daughter of Serge' Gainsbourg's 5:55 album, there's a fascinating song called 'The Operation'. Written by Jarvis Cocker, it compares a relationship to heart surgery. 'Our love goes under the knife,' breathes Gainsbourg, in the kind of voice that tends to cause palpitations. 'The heart was rejected by the host.'

For most lyricists, of course, the heart isn't a slippery, fist-sized lump of muscle at all. It's love and life and soul. These hearts don't just beat; they leap, they soar, they melt, they burst, they ache, they break, they shatter, they stop. On occasion, they are totally eclipsed.

Lest we forget, the heartbeat is also the basis of rhythm. The narrator of Wire's tense two-chord throb obsessively chants along to his internal metronome: 'I am mesmerised by my own beat.' In 'Heartbeat' by Norwegian pop star Annie, the music also enacts the lyrics. As Annie describes falling in love at a party, the drums thump out her racing pulse.

Its title may carry disturbing implications of vascular disease, and its sentiments may be pure emotional masochism, but 'This Old Heart of Mine (Is Weak for You)' is thunderously alive: one of Motown's greatest love songs. 'Heart of Glass' began as a genre exercise – the demo version bore the mundane subtitle 'The Disco

Song' – and ended up as Blondie's most enduring hit. Poised between disco and punk, Debbie Harry swoops from an airy, Donna Summer-esque trill ('once had a love . . .') to earthy, gum-chewing realism ('pain in the ass') in the space of four bars. There's another faulty organ causing problems in the Magnetic Fields' painfully frank 'I Think I Need a New Heart'.

It's possible to make a meal of a song without making people throw up. Produced by Trevor Horn, ABC's 'All of My Heart' is as lavishly crammed as a Valentine's Day box of chocolates but it's also a masterclass in precision, with not a single keyboard curlicue or orchestral ornament out of place. No less showstopping is Janis Joplin's tour de force reading of 'Piece of My Heart'. Erma Franklin's original version is great too, but Joplin's has a ragged, end-of-the-night intensity all its own.

We're travelling deep into heartache country now. Thanks to the Honest Jon's label, the reputation of southern soul singer Bettye Swann has been justly revived. In this, her finest moment, she lowers the shutters on her wounded heart and lets it languish, as sad and empty as a holiday resort in winter. Meanwhile, in Kate and Anna McGarrigle's weapons-grade break-up song, the heart is a buckled wheel and a sinking ship. 'It's only love that can wreck a human being and turn him inside out,' they harmonise, like disconsolate angels. There's just time to plunge into the oceanic sadness of Spiritualized's 'Broken Heart', in the midst of which Jason Pierce's matter-of-fact humour ('I'm too busy to be heartbroken') serves as a small but exceedingly welcome life raft.

THE PLAYLIST

Heartbeat Wire

Heartbeat Annie

This Old Heart of Mine (Is Weak for You) The Isley Brothers

Heart of Glass Blondie

I Think I Need a New Heart The Magnetic Fields

All of My Heart ABC

Piece of My Heart Janis Joplin

(My Heart Is) Closed for the Season Bettye Swann

Heart like a Wheel Kate and Anna McGarrigle

Broken Heart Spiritualized

NEW YORK

(▶) There's a famous *New Yorker* cartoon, entitled 'View of the World from 9th Avenue', in which everything west of the Hudson River is an irrelevant blur. It both spoofs and flatters New Yorkers' conviction, expressed in John Dos Passos's *Manhattan Transfer* (the novel, not the authorised biography of the 1970s jazz-pop combo), that their town is 'the centre of things'. Whether you're listening to Leonard Bernstein's 'New York, New York' or BDP's hip-hop creation myth 'South Bronx', you'll hear the same message: this is the only city that counts. When it comes to pop music, from Broadway and the Brill Building to disco, punk and rap, they have a point.

Our first tour guides to the five boroughs are Rodgers and Hart, via Ella Fitzgerald. This song is as swish and old-fashioned as a carriage ride through Central Park. The Ramones were sharply attuned to New York's dark side ('53rd & 3rd' is all razor blades and rent boys), which makes their ode to summer on Long Island's south shore sound even sweeter.

Next, two urban love stories. They Might Be Giants usually exceed my quirk quotient by about a million per cent but this zingy cover of Cub's 'New York City' is charm itself: 'The best thing about New

York City is you and me.' 'You Said Something' is just one slice of Gotham romance from P.J. Harvey's NY-themed *Stories from the City, Stories from the Sea*, which had the misfortune to win the Mercury Prize on, of all days, 11 September 2001. Harvey surveys the New York skyline with an outsider's eyes, but for a local's perspective you can't beat Odyssey's bittersweet disco classic. It feels like Times Square on a Saturday night.

110th Street is the northern border of Central Park, where Manhattan hands over to Harlem, knowledge I owe entirely to Bobby Womack, and his bleak, beautiful expression of ghetto angst. What soul began, hip-hop continued. *Illmatic*, the debut from Queens rapper Nas, is the definitive New York rap album, bustling with dense, vivid narratives like 'NY State of Mind'.

Only the boldest or cockiest songwriters attempt to bottle the city's bubbling variety in just one song. Grace Jones sets Melvin Van Peebles's colourful prose poem to lilting reggae: 'No it ain't World War Four / It's just the apple stretching and yawning.' Having mythologised New York his whole career, Lou Reed finally devoted a whole album to it in 1989. 'Dirty Blvd' is the sour standout track: a glimpse of urban hell.

Despite the brow-straining efforts of Bruce Springsteen et al, I'm not sure any song can add much to our perception of what happened to New York on 9/11, but music can still strike a chord. In the days surrounding the first anniversary, a friend of mine in Manhattan listened obsessively to Interpol's just-released 'NYC', and I could see why. It sounds like a wake, but a rebirth too.

THE PLAYLIST

Manhattan Ella Fitzgerald
Rockaway Beach The Ramones
New York City They Might Be Giants
You Said Something P.J. Harvey
Native New Yorker Odyssey
Across 110th Street Bobby Womack
NY State of Mind Nas
The Apple Stretching Grace Jones
Dirty Blvd Lou Reed
NYC Interpol

CALIFORNIA

▶ Sacramento-born writer Joan Didion memorably described California as 'troubled by some buried but ineradicable suspicion that things had better work here, because here, beneath that immense bleached sky, is where we run out of continent'. People have always come to California looking for something, whether it's money, sunshine, fame or freedom: basically, a new start. If, like Horace Greeley and the Village People, you believe that the great American imperative is 'Go west!', then California, for good or ill, is the end of the road.

No wonder some songwriters glorify the state (the Red Hot Chili Peppers would have you believe that injecting smack is intrinsically more glamorous if it takes place under a bridge in Los Angeles rather than, say, Duluth), while others damn it with equal passion. It's a hard place to be lukewarm about.

We start, as if compelled by law, with the Mamas and the Papas' sublime love letter home. Thirty years prior, Woody Guthrie questioned the Californian ideal with 'Do-Re-Mi', in which weary dustbowl refugees come flocking to this 'garden of Eden' only to find yet more struggle. Chuck Berry's rock 'n' roll picaresque 'Promised Land' has a happier ending. Berry wrote it while incarcerated, using an atlas from the prison library to plot his hero's itinerary from Virginia to LA.

Love were such pariahs on LA's Sunset Strip in the 1960s that a rival musician contemptuously rechristened them Hate. This song, named after the stretch which housed the Whiskey-A-Go-Go club, is upbeat yet uneasy, as if sensing the madness waiting around the corner. Charles Manson, madness incarnate, later inspired 'Revolution Blues', Neil Young's troubling, lunatic's-eye view of LA's cloistered millionaire hippies (himself included): 'Well I hear that Laurel Canyon is full of famous stars / But I hate them worse than lepers and I'll kill them in their cars.'

Manson makes a cameo appearance in NWA's 'Straight Outta Compton'. All at once, it is a scorching malcontent's battle cry on a par with 'Anarchy in the UK'; a hard-nosed statement of local identity which placed an unremarkable LA suburb at the centre of the hip-hop universe; gangsta rap's ground zero; and a deathlessly exciting racket.

If California is a place of promises made and betrayed, then Hollywood is its spiritual capital. John Lydon looms over it like a cackling wraith on Leftfield's 'Open Up', updating Public Enemy's cry of 'burn Hollywood burn', while Dionne Warwick is the disappointed starlet heading home in Bacharach and David's poignant 'Do You Know the Way to San Jose?': 'Weeks turn into years and quickly pass / All the stars there never were are parking cars and pumping gas.'

And so we heard north. In 'Unfair', Stockton-based Pavement chart their divided state, from Mount Shasta and Santa Rosa down to Lake Tahoe and Bakersfield, protesting that 'the south takes what the north delivers'. Up in San Francisco Bay, a heartsick Otis Redding ends his 2000-mile trek, because here, beneath that immense bleached sky, is where he runs out of continent.

THE PLAYLIST

California Dreamin' The Mamas and the Papas
Do-Re-Mi Woody Guthrie
Promised Land Chuck Berry
Maybe the People Would Be the Times or Between Clark and Hilldale Love
Revolution Blues Neil Young
Straight Outta Compton NWA
Open Up (Full Vocal Mix) Leftfield
Do You Know the Way to San Jose? Dionne Warwick
Unfair Pavement
(Sittin' on) the Dock of the Bay Otis Redding

ONE-NIGHT STANDS

(▶) Readers of a certain newspaper may be familiar with a weekly column called 'Sleeping Around', which details, at some length, the adventures of a woman who seemingly can't pop out for a pint of milk without indulging in hot hot sex. The remarkable thing about it is the gulf between the activity itself (fun, presumably) and the shattering tedium of the consequent prose.

As the enduring popularity of the *Literary Review*'s Bad Sex award proves, writing about sex tends to be either dull or embarrassing, so it makes sense that the best songs deal not with the prosaic business of who did what to whom but with the messy tangle of emotions – guilt, desperation, regret – which often attends one-night stands. If you can do both well, then you're probably Leonard Cohen.

We start with some simple, unapologetic cock-rock. AC/DC's Brian Johnson recounts a seismic fling with an endearing blend of gratitude and awe. He's an old-fashioned romantic next to Rod Stewart on the Faces' knowingly rogueish 'Stay With Me', callous in the verses yet weirdly needy in the chorus. Quite the catch, ladies.

Prince's graphic 'Darling Nikki' has the fantastical quality of a letter to an adult magazine: 'Dear Penthouse Forum, I used to think your letters were made up but the other day I met this girl in a hotel lobby . . .' If he had dated Grace Jones, they could have generated enough sexual voltage to power the eastern seaboard, judging by the cackling innuendo of 'Pull Up to the Bumper'.

Back when I didn't listen to lyrics properly, I assumed that the Psychedelic Furs' biggest hit was just about someone who looked, y'know, pretty in pink. The pre-Molly Ringwald 1981 version, with its ominous drone and snarling vocals, grants the theme of desperate promiscuity a bleaker edge. Liz Phair sings 'Fuck and Run' like she's just stumbled out of bed, mingling weary regret with grumpy embarrassment that she desires more. 'I want a boyfriend,' she sighs. 'I want all that stupid old shit.' The Aloof's Ricky Barrow is beyond hope on the magnificently self-loathing electronic soul of 'One Night Stand'. Desolate to the core, it's enough to put you off sex for life.

Being left by husband André for Mia Farrow in 1969 did wonders for Dory Previn's songwriting. 'Lady with the Braid' is an exquisitely observed study of the mindset of the reluctantly single: 'Would you care to stay till sunrise? / It's completely your decision / It's just the night cuts through me like a knife.' Songwriters Gerry Goffin and Carole King reduce the same anxiety to one simple inquiry on the Shirelles' 'Will You Love Me Tomorrow'.

Lest we get too depressed, we'll end on an upbeat note. Written by Chip Taylor, 'Angel of the Morning' has been covered by everyone from Nina Simone to Howard from the Halifax ads. P.P. Arnold's is arguably the best. It's the indomitable pride with which she declares

'I won't beg you to stay with me', the vibrant determination to appreciate the night for what it was, whatever happens next.

THE PLAYLIST

You Shook Me All Night Long AC/DC
Stay With Me The Faces
Darling Nikki Prince
Pull Up to the Bumper Grace Jones
Pretty in Pink The Psychedelic Furs
Fuck and Run Liz Phair
One Night Stand The Aloof
The Lady with the Braid Dory Previn
Will You Love Me Tomorrow The Shirelles
Angel of the Morning P.P. Arnold

FATHERS

▶ Becoming a parent and losing one are two of life's seismic events. Perhaps it's their sheer enormity that makes them such tricky subjects, often stunning songwriters into either sanctimony or schmaltz. When I hear Harry Chapin's 'Cat's in the Cradle' or Luther Vandross's 'Dance with my Father', I hear genuine emotion curdling into kitsch.

Pop music's worst father is surely the one featured in the Temptations' 'Papa Was a Rollin' Stone': corrupt preacher, philandering alcoholic and five-star cad. Exquisitely crafted by Motown visionary Norman Whitfield, this masterpiece of smouldering tension has proved invaluable to any sub-editor seeking a headline for a Jade Jagger story. Two more from the dark side: Aphex Twin unleashes punk-techno hell on 'Come to Daddy' and Morrissey tells the story of a patriarch's perplexing speech defect.

Most new dads only get to bore their friends, but the proud rock star dad can annoy the whole world. One of the few truly likeable songs about fatherhood is David Bowie's jaunty, self-effacing 'Kooks', although advising 'Don't pick fights with the bullies or the cads' is a bit rich from someone who christened the poor bugger Zowie, thus giving bullies and cads the green light. Another newborn, Noah Yorke, inspired Radiohead's end-of-the-world lullaby 'Sail to the

Moon': 'In the flood you'll build an ark / And sail us to the moon.' For a different take on paternity and destiny, try John Fogerty's 'Fortunate Son', a howl of blue-collar indignation directed at the privileged elite who used their connections to shield their offspring from the Vietnam draft.

The self-satisfied tone of Cat Stevens' 'Father and Son' has always rubbed me the wrong way, so let's have 'A Father and a Son' by Loudon Wainwright III instead. This poignant reflection on why generations clash ('I don't know about this Oedipal stuff / But when we were together it was always rough') was inspired by his father's death. His children, Rufus and Martha, have continued the family tradition of airing their dirty laundry in the studio by writing unflattering songs about Loudon. Man hands on misery to man . . .

If the Temptations' useless papa had repented before he died, he might have sounded like the protagonist of Pulp's wrenching 'A Little Soul', a man so hobbled by guilt that he thinks his son is better off without him: 'You look like me but please don't turn out like me.' Ian Dury's 'My Old Man' is far sweeter: a funny, affectionate remembrance of his dad, an East End bus driver. At Dury's funeral in 2000, the song was performed by his own son, Baxter.

There are several songs about mourning a father, among them the Streets' 'Never Went to Church', but none puts a lump in the throat as reliably as Billy Bragg's 'Tank Park Salute'. Written as a way of addressing the silence and denial that shrouded his dad's illness, it resonates with the desperate sadness of things unsaid and whispers to the listener: *Don't make the same mistake.*

THE PLAYLIST

Papa Was a Rollin' Stone The Temptations

Come to Daddy Aphex Twin

Don't Make Fun of Daddy's Voice Morrissey

Kooks David Bowie

Sail to the Moon Radiohead

Fortunate Son Creedence Clearwater Revival

A Father and a Son Loudon Wainwright III

A Little Soul Pulp

My Old Man Ian Dury

Tank Park Salute Billy Bragg

SONGS ABOUT
MOTHERS

(▶) If pop is anything to go by (and if it isn't then I've been living my life all wrong), then mothers beat fathers hands down. There is no 'Mama Was a Rolling Stone' or 'Mama Don't Preach'. Next to the deadbeats and tyrants that stalk musical depictions of fatherhood, mothers are loving, saintly, all-knowing and, at worst, gently disapproving. Apart from Eminem's mum, who, if her son is to be believed, is a hateful witch.

Some mothers are influential in their absence: Lennon, McCartney, Hendrix, Bono and Madonna all lost their mums before the age of eighteen. In fact Julia Lennon might just be the most celebrated mother in pop. Even if you miss the message of the Beatles' 'Julia', then the Plastic Ono Band's 'Mother' and 'My Mummy's Dead' should clear things up.

Pop mothers are inexhaustible sources of zen counsel. Doris Day's assured her that whatever will be will be, Junior's told him not to rush to grow old, and the Shirelles' mama, on this slice of girl-group perfection, warned that 'there'll be days like this'. Next, two very modern scenarios: a gay son inviting his mum on a messy weekender ('Take Your Mama'), and a separated dad saying sorry to his 'baby mama's mama' ('Ms Jackson'), although Big Boi's indignant verses suggest that it's a qualified apology.

Kate Bush's heart-shuddering worry in 'This Woman's Work' means different things to different people – it could be about giving birth to a child or raising one – but the song's swelling beauty requires no explanation. Natalie Merchant's pregnant narrator in 'Eat for Two' is also wracked with anxiety: 'I walk for two? I'm stumbling / Breathe for two? I can't breathe.'

For an abrupt change of pace, here's Can's thrumming, pagan trance-rock, centred on Damo Suzuki's woozy incantation, 'I say mothers ain't too cool like mother sky.' There are literally hundreds of versions of the slavery-era spiritual 'Sometimes I Feel Like a Motherless Child'; I'm a fan of O.V. Wright's emotionally poleaxing southern soul rendition, a performance worthy of Otis Redding.

Few events can make your world implode like the death of a mother – consider the Carter Family's 'Will the Circle Be Unbroken' or the Durutti Column's wrenching 'Requiem for My Mother'. Gram Parsons fondly remembers the minutiae of his mum's life on 'Brass Buttons', while Big Star's Alex Chilton describes the death of his girlfriend's mother, in language that cuts to the core of bereavement with its shocking loss of perspective, as a holocaust.

Hip-hop is not renowned for its sentimentality, but even the most hardened hustler becomes a mushy-hearted sap where his mum is concerned. Rap's greatest lip-trembler is 'All That I Got Is You', its lachrymose Jackson 5 sample rubbing against Ghostface Killah's admirably frank memories of his flawed but loving single mother.

When Mary J. Blige swoops in, playing the part of Ma Killah, there's not a dry eye in my house.

THE PLAYLIST

Mama Said The Shirelles
Take Your Mama Scissor Sisters
Ms Jackson OutKast
This Woman's Work Kate Bush
Eat for Two 10,000 Maniacs
Mother Sky Can
Motherless Child O.V. Wright
Brass Buttons Gram Parsons
Holocaust Big Star
All That I Got Is You Ghostface Killah

MORNING
SONGS

(▶) At an impressionable age, I was indelibly marked by a bank advert in which an artfully dishevelled loft-dweller ventured out at daybreak to buy milk for his cat to the strains of 'Easy' by the Commodores. All his neighbours thought he was the business. *Yes*, I thought. *That's what adult life will be like.*

I've never lived in a loft and I'm allergic to cats, but at least I've had plenty of morning soundtracks. I've woken up for days in a row to Saint Etienne's 'Mario's Café'; sat outside a lousy hotel in Seattle, chain-smoking to Kris Kristofferson's majestically bleak 'Sunday Morning Coming Down'; and met the dawn, dazed from lack of sleep, with Nina Simone's version of 'Here Comes the Sun'. Whether it's a wondrous morning or a humdrum one, it's good to mark it with a song.

Let's start with an instrumental. The Sabres of Paradise's *Haunted Dancehall* is a techno-dub sort-of-concept album, tracing a winding path through London's nocturnal backstreets. Towards the end, 'Jacob Street 7 a.m.' shimmers like a cold dawn, shivery and pale, but with the promise of something magical.

From London SE1 to New York's Chelsea, where the sun pours in like butterscotch, the traffic rings out like Christmas bells and a young Joni Mitchell tingles with possibility. Then back across the Atlantic to Paris 1966, and the morning routine of Tunisian teenager Jacqueline Taïeb. There's an English-language version too, clarifying such pressing concerns as her missing toothbrush and her crush on Paul McCartney, but this beat-pop wake-up call sounds much more glamorous *en français*.

Dusty Springfield classily proposes an exceptional start to the day on 'Just a Little Lovin', although if that's too understated you can have 'a proper wriggle in the naughty naked nude' to Ian Dury's 'Wake Up and Make Love with Me'. Next, two metaphorical mornings. A battered but unbowed Gil Scott-Heron announces a fresh start on 'I Think I'll Call It Morning', while 'Pure Morning', a song that makes Placebo-haters do a double-take, is a thunderous, mantric ode to companionship. You could raise a militia to this song.

Some mornings are tougher than others. The Cowboy Junkies' Margo Timmins tackles life after heartbreak with a bleary, conversational narrative that sounds as if she's improvising it while waking up, her thoughts meandering from coffee to Coltrane to the extra space in her bed. (For a flintier alternative, try the Dresden Dolls' startling 'First Orgasm'.) Then there's Scottish folk singer James Yorkston, struggling to rise at 6.30. The supple, slow-building music seems to take your hand from beneath the duvet and lead you outside.

In Pulp's 'Sunrise', a raver repents. 'You've been awake all night, so why should you crash out at dawn?', demands Jarvis Cocker, summoning a cleansing storm of pagan psychedelia. The closing song on Pulp's final album, it's a swansong that sounds like a rebirth. After that, we touch down with the Velvet Underground's immaculate, inevitable 'Sunday Morning', laced with paranoia but as soft as a prayer.

THE PLAYLIST

Jacob Street 7 a.m. The Sabres of Paradise

Chelsea Morning Joni Mitchell

7 Heures du Matin Jacqueline Taïeb

Just a Little Lovin' Dusty Springfield

I Think I'll Call It Morning Gil Scott-Heron

Pure Morning Placebo

Sun Comes Up, It's Tuesday Morning Cowboy Junkies

6.30 Is Just Way Too Early James Yorkston and the Athletes

Sunrise Pulp

Sunday Morning The Velvet Underground

HEAT

(▶) Music can do more than chime with your surroundings; it can transform them. A good hot-weather record enhances a feeling that's already there; a great one can make even members of the British Antarctic Survey feel like changing into shorts and sandals and making cocktails with little umbrellas in them.

The British always seem taken unawares by summer. They don't quite know what to do with themselves, which is why, on the first hot day of the year, the country suddenly sprouts a legion of lobster-hued, bare-chested men getting drunk at midday and messing up barbecues. Noël Coward famously recorded the behaviour of mad dogs and Englishmen, and the Fall offer their own fractured observations on the topic: 'Do they know they can get cancer? / Designer tramp goes grrr / Looking jolly from Stoke.' It's catchy.

If the weather won't oblige, then raise the temperature by other means. Martha Reeves and the Vandellas heralded the desire-crazed 'Heat Wave' with one of the greatest intros in pop. Too sultry to do much more than fan the bugs away and sip her mint julep, Peggy Lee delivers a wry treatise on the theme: 'Cats were born to give chicks fever / Be it Fahrenheit or centigrade.' Nobody who's covered it since, least of all the mirthless Madonna, has nailed the song's insouciant humour quite like Lee.

Sexual heat becomes sinister on Siouxsie and the Banshees' 'Melt!', a clammy fever dream of blazing orchids and deliquescing lovers. On 'Hot Head's churning bizarro-blues, Captain Beefheart takes the usual hot-love clichés to deliriously literal extremes: 'She can boil a pot o' Joe / She can start a pile o' dough.' Snoop Dogg, scourge of right-thinking society turned lovable catchphrase-manufacturer, sounds like he thought up 'Drop It Like It's Hot's title first, then had to contrive a song around it, and why not? The Neptunes' beat bounces like a ping-pong ball.

While records like 'Summer Breeze' celebrate a balmy day, others capture the oppressive fug of an airless one. The Drifters sought refuge up on the roof and under the boardwalk but the Lovin' Spoonful waited till nightfall. As the tension breaks on the chorus, you share their relief. Dub maestro Lee 'Scratch' Perry proposes escaping to the countryside, but the music's humid crawl makes you doubt he'll find the energy. The Triffids' 'Too Hot to Move, Too Hot to Think' is a dreamy, perturbing survey of an Australian city at night: 'No one gets much sleeping done / Till they've been crying through and through.'

When most rock stars unravel, there's usually some kind of warning; Brian Wilson's mental collapse was foreshadowed by the melancholy undertow of his earlier work. But nothing on Sly Stone's 1960s albums hinted at the loneliness and lethargy that would define the subsequent decade. 'Hot Fun in the Summertime', his last single before 'There's a Riot Goin' On', is incandescent with childlike optimism. If you must get drunk and botch a barbecue, then you might as well do it to this.

THE PLAYLIST

British People in Hot Weather The Fall

Heat Wave Martha Reeves and the Vandellas

Fever Peggy Lee

Melt! Siouxsie and the Banshees

Hot Head Captain Beefheart

Drop It Like It's Hot Snoop Dogg feat. Pharrell

Summer in the City The Lovin' Spoonful

City Too Hot Lee 'Scratch' Perry

Too Hot to Move, Too Hot to Think The Triffids

Hot Fun in the Summertime Sly and the Family Stone

SONGS ABOUT
DEATH

(▶) In the film *High Fidelity*, a trio of music buffs who know more about pop than they do about life respond to a friend's bereavement by compiling a list of songs about death. One suggestion is overruled because it appeared in *The Big Chill*. By the same logic, I've disqualified anything named in *High Fidelity*. The characters would understand.

The joke is that these emotional pygmies can only process life's big events via music but surely that's as good a way as any to deal with the prospect of oblivion. All art helps to ward off nothingness, and the most insightful treatments of the subject sharpen the senses, like the slaves assigned to whisper in the ears of victorious Roman generals: 'Remember thou art mortal.'

Most recent songs about death deal with bereavement, which merits its own playlist. Thoughts of one's own mortality are not as widespread as they were when war and pestilence were busily curtailing life expectancy. A collection of old folk songs is a musical mortuary, piled high with unfortunates. 'O Death', a traditional Appalachian song performed *a cappella* by septuagenarian Ralph Stanley for the *O Brother, Where Art Thou?* soundtrack, has that authentic whiff of the boneyard.

On Depeche Mode's shiny goth-funk monolith 'Fly on the Windscreen', Dave Gahan wails 'death is everywhere' as if the thought had just that second occurred to him, before cunningly employing this revelation as a seduction ploy. Muse's dying atheist is caught between his terror of the void and his panic that maybe another realm does exist after all.

Time for a glimmer of light. Blue Öyster Cult's psychedelic hard-rock classic offers reassurance with a vision of lovers united in the afterlife, but then Sparks wittily imagine a disgruntled Romeo whose Juliet reneged on the deal: 'It is hell knowing that your health will keep you out of here / For many, many years.' Still, at least there's a 'panoramic view'.

The next two songs are delivered from beyond the grave. In the traditional 'When I Was on Horseback', performed with spectral grace by Steeleye Span, an Irish cavalryman bemoans his premature demise. Blind Lemon Jefferson's narrator asks only that his resting place is well tended, but life supplied a cruel footnote. When Jefferson died two years after recording it, he didn't even get a headstone.

Finally (and finally is an apt word), three which are not what they seem. Jacques Brel's 'My Death' fashions thoughts of extinction into a towering love song, its morbid romance fitting Scott Walker's voice as snugly as a deathmask. Bonnie 'Prince' Billy's tomb-cold 'Death to Everyone' may feel like bony fingers on your shoulder but its lyrics are a *carpe diem* manifesto: 'Since we know our end will come / It makes our living fun.' Conversely, Nick Cave and his all-star choir of the damned give Bob Dylan's spiritual bromide 'Death Is Not the End' a mischievously bleak twist. There is no peace: the hard times just continue on the other side.

THE PLAYLIST

O Death Ralph Stanley
Fly on the Windscreen (Final) Depeche Mode
Thoughts of a Dying Atheist Muse
(Don't Fear) the Reaper Blue Öyster Cult
Here in Heaven Sparks
When I Was on Horseback Steeleye Span
See That My Grave is Kept Clean Blind Lemon Jefferson
My Death Scott Walker
Death to Everyone Bonnie 'Prince' Billy
Death Is Not the End Nick Cave and the Bad Seeds

SPOKEN-WORD
SONGS

(▶) Promoting his Edgar Allan Poe-inspired folly *The Raven* five years ago, Lou Reed protested: 'It's not spoken word. Spoken word sounds like a biography of Winston Churchill read to you by Ian McKellen . . . [People] want spoken word like they want an amputated foot.' Leaving aside the fact that a biography of Churchill read by McKellen, or indeed an amputated foot, would be more enjoyable than *The Raven*, Reed had a point.

Spoken word is intrusive. It bends your ear. It demands your attention whether it deserves it or not. Even the good stuff can lose its allure pretty rapidly. Take Dan Le Sac vs Scroobius Pip's 2007 MySpace sensation, 'Thou Shalt Not Kill': funny the first time you hear it, not so endearing the fourth or fifth, positively maddening by the tenth.

Here are ten spoken-word songs that I think repay the effort. I've excluded novelty records, rapping, dialogue sampled from other sources, and tracks such as 'Once in a Lifetime' and 'West End Girls', which are structured as regular songs, no matter how conversational the delivery.

First, some politics. Prince Buster's tongue-in-cheek response to rampant crime in 1960s Jamaica was the character of Judge Dread, a bullish justice handing down 400-year sentences to hapless rude boys. The young Gil Scott-Heron had the lot: anger, empathy, lancing wit and the ability to make words dance. This is an obvious choice but an undeniable one: conscious hip-hop long before the fact.

The teenage melodramas of 1960s girl groups thrived on spoken interludes, but the Shangri-Las' strangest hit permits no melodic release, just the halting testimony of a girl numbed by some unspecified romantic tragedy (perhaps a rape) and terrified of love. Serge Gainsbourg's classic song cycle *Histoire de Melody Nelson* begins with a fateful car accident, framed by the most glorious music he ever composed.

Should 'O Superman' be here? Laurie Anderson based it on a Jules Massenet aria and she sings in places, but how else would you define this disorientating, DeLillo-esque reflection on communication and the military-industrial complex? For Talking Heads' David Byrne, singing and talking overlapped, but 'Seen and Not Seen' is definitely the latter: doubt and disconnection set to flickering funk.

From Byrne's pristine alienation to John Cooper Clarke's reeking urban nightmares. Arctic Monkeys cite him as an influence but even their jaundiced outlook on the urban north seems happy-clappy beside the grimy despair of 'Beasley Street'. Stormclouds gather during 'Good Morning, Captain' by post-rock forefathers Slint, until Brian MacMahon's mumbled *Ancient Mariner*-inspired narration finally bursts into a primitive howl of 'I miss you!'

For some reason, Scottish performers are especially drawn to spoken word. Just elbowing out Arab Strap and Belle and Sebastian, Ballboy's 'A Day in Space' is a whimsical manifesto for thinking big. To end on, an extract from Ivor Cutler's aural memoirs, distinguished by gorse-dry humour and the spectral drone of a harmonium. Not much happens – a childhood walk in the icy outdoors, then a welcome return home to pink cheeks and cooking smells – but it is enough.

THE PLAYLIST

Judge Dread Prince Buster
The Revolution Will Not Be Televised Gil Scott-Heron
Past, Present and Future The Shangri-Las
Melody Serge Gainsbourg
O Superman Laurie Anderson
Seen and Not Seen Talking Heads
Beasley Street John Cooper Clarke
Good Morning, Captain Slint
A Day in Space Ballboy
Life in a Scotch Sitting Room, #2, Episode 11 Ivor Cutler

INSTRUMENTALS

(▶) Instrumentals get a raw deal from some listeners. Outside of genres such as jazz, classical or techno, the absence of that most evocative instrument, the human voice, is often deemed a failing. One thinks of cheerful novelty records or half-hearted album fillers – they are nobody's desert island discs.

Of course, there is ample evidence to the contrary, but an instrumental has to work harder, to be more ingenious in its pace and construction, if it wants to hook the listener. Although I'll happily drift off to Brian Eno's ambient albums – music designed not to demand attention – I've chosen pieces that can hold their own in any company.

The job is hardest if you are famed for songs: think of Radiohead's trifling 'Treefingers' or the Beatles' forgettable 'Flying'. The Small Faces aimed higher when raising the curtain on their concept album *Ogdens' Nut Gone Flake* with a widescreen theme tune for a London waking up to its first blast of psychedelic sunshine.

Instrumentals favour loose coalitions of anonymous session musicians and industry insiders. Mr Bloe scored their sole hit with a harmonica-driven romp for which I remember my dad nurturing an unwavering passion, and A&R man Michael Viner granted the Shadows an improbable place in hip-hop history when his ad hoc

Incredible Bongo Band gave their 1960 hit 'Apache' a walloping breakbeat and marvelled as it became a ubiquitous South Bronx soundtrack.

Link Wray's 'Rumble' holds the honour of being the only instrumental barred from radio playlists for encouraging juvenile delinquency, which is testament to its ominous drama – hard not to picture flick-knives and bike-chains. Pete Townshend credits its streetwalking power chords with making him first pick up a guitar. Not long afterwards, maverick guitarist Davy Graham's sinuous tribute to his girlfriend Angi had a seismic impact on the growth of folk-rock.

Before Bowie's Berlin albums, major rock artists used instrumentals as intros, outros or interludes: side dishes. He made them the main course, or at least dessert, taking tips from Kraftwerk, Neu! and collaborator Brian Eno. At first tentative, then robustly optimistic, 'A New Career in a New Town' is the sound of self-rediscovery. Tracks like this doubtless inspired Simple Minds to craft the majestic 'Theme for Great Cities': shivery synths dawning over icebound funk. Then they settled for being U2's blowhard understudies. What a waste.

If we must pick a single tune to represent jazz – and I'm afraid we must – then 'So What' can shoulder the weight better than most. It's famous for good reason: so bewitching and agile that overexposure cannot dim its charms. Flying the flag for dance music is Hardfloor's unadulterated acid house. There's just one instrument apart from the drum machine: the Roland TB-303 synthesiser, driven to fresh heights of delirium.

Some examples of post-rock – that microphone-shunning genre birthed in the early 1990s – are so dreary they make you beg for vocal relief. Certain Mogwai tracks are guilty, but 'Mogwai Fear Satan's vast tides of guitar, now surging, now sighing, leave me speechless.

THE PLAYLIST

Ogdens' Nut Gone Flake The Small Faces
Groovin' with Mr Bloe Mr Bloe
Apache The Incredible Bongo Band
Rumble Link Wray
Angi Davy Graham
A New Career in a New Town David Bowie
Theme for Great Cities Simple Minds
So What Miles Davis
Acperience I Hardfloor
Mogwai Fear Satan Mogwai

OTHER MUSICIANS

(▶) Just as soap opera characters don't wind down by watching soap operas, songwriters rarely acknowledge each other's existence in song unless they're personally acquainted. So when they do, they reveal at least as much about themselves as their subjects, whether they're acknowledging inspirations (the Fall's 'I Am Damo Suzuki'); saluting fallen greats (Neil Young's 'Sleeps with Angels', about Kurt Cobain); parsing rock history (Drive-By Truckers' 'Ronnie and Neil'); mocking perceived foes (Mojo Nixon's 'Don Henley Must Die'); or – how to put this? – admiring non-musical attributes (the Saw Doctors' 'I'd Love to Bang the Bangles').

Dexy's Midnight Runners appeared out of a clear blue sky, with a sound and manifesto – 'soul power' – all their own. Nobody else in pop's class of 1980 would have dreamt of producing an impassioned, brass-powered tribute to neglected 1960s soul singer Geno Washington, let alone taken it to number one. It's not their fault that it instantly outshone everything Washington had recorded. When Wham! split up, Andrew Ridgley's name quickly became a punchline to jokes about pop's hapless Other Blokes, but Black Box Recorder's song is an unexpectedly sincere homage to 1980s sidemen and the volcanic power of the teenage crush: 'I never liked George Michael much / Although they say he was the talented one.'

LCD Soundsystem imagine a fan saving for seven years to book the world's hippest Frenchmen for his house party, and remixers Soulwax go one better, cleverly dropping in snatches of Daft Punk's own tracks so that the record sounds like the very event it describes. Likewise, Jonathan Richman performs a few bars of the Velvet Underground's 'Sister Ray' in his best Lou Reed voice, in between dispensing eloquent insights into his heroes' dark magic: 'Bold and brash, stark and still / Like the heating's off and you can't pay the bill.' (The Rockingbirds later honoured Richman with 'Jonathan, Jonathan'. Alas, nobody has yet sung about the Rockingbirds.)

Things get weirder as Jeffrey Lewis imagines a disturbing encounter with alt-country icon Will Oldham in a hoarse, manic ramble, like he's just woken up and is trying to describe a dream before he forgets it. As a brutally candid portrait of artistic self-doubt ('I kinda thought I was gonna grow up to do stuff that would benefit humanity'), it is simply extraordinary. Meanwhile, Smog's Bill Callahan pictures the king of Paisley Park as a lonely, ascetic perfectionist, and Sonic Youth's Kim Gordon casts herself as Karen Carpenter reporting back from heaven, splicing dreamy observations ('Hello Janis, hello Dennis, Elvis') with disturbing reminders of the anorexia that killed her.

Three personal notes to end on. Bowie gave his friend Marc Bolan the thinnest of disguises as the titular 'Lady Stardust' (it was originally titled 'Song for Marc'), John Martyn extended a concerned hand to a waning Nick Drake on the devastatingly tender 'Solid Air', and Charles Mingus demonstrated his affection for tragic saxophonist Lester Young the way he knew best, with this sublime elegy. If only we could all inspire such a send-off.

THE PLAYLIST

Geno Dexy's Midnight Runners

Andrew Ridgley Black Box Recorder

Daft Punk Is Playing at My House (Soulwax Shibuya Daft mix) LCD Soundsystem

Velvet Underground Jonathan Richman

Williamsburg Will Oldham Horror Jeffrey and Jack Lewis

Prince Alone in the Studio Smog

Tunic (Song for Karen) Sonic Youth

Lady Stardust David Bowie

Solid Air John Martyn

Goodbye Pork Pie Hat Charles Mingus

POLITICIANS

(▶) Never let it be said that popular song isn't educational. If not for a certain wartime singalong, how else would we have discovered that Hitler had but a single testicle and Goering had two that were very small? Or, furthermore, that Himmler had something similar, while Goebbels had no balls at all?

Politicians provide artists with a rich cast of heroes and villains to choose from. I suspect the White House's current occupant has been damned in song more often even than Nixon, and at least one industry that boomed under Thatcher was the manufacture of protest songs. Other statesmen are niche interests, among them ill-fated Democratic presidential candidate Adlai Stevenson (Sufjan Stevens), Romanian tyrant Nicolae Ceausescu (Fatima Mansions) and assassinated British PM Spencer Perceval (iLiKETRAiNS).

During Reagan's second term, REM sensed the malign spirit of notorious red-baiter Joe McCarthy at work, dropping in a sample of army attorney Joseph Welch taking the old bully to task in 1954. Another, even more loathsome dead Joe haunts the landscape of Scott Walker's exquisitely orchestrated 'The Old Man's Back Again', inspired by the Prague spring of 1968 and the subsequent Soviet crackdown. The clunky subtitle was presumably appended lest anyone think the old man in question was not Stalin but Clive Dunn.

You could construct whole compilations devoted to savaging Nixon and Thatcher. By 1974, Stevie Wonder had already written 'Misstra Know-It-All', but the mordant 'You Haven't Done Nothin'' had the advantage of timing. Two weeks after Wonder crowed 'You brought this upon yourself,' Nixon resigned. Conversely, 'Stand Down Margaret' came at the turbulent dawn of the Thatcher era, that unexpected 'please' packing a fiercely ironic punch. After re-forming in 2005, the Beat amended it to 'Stand Down Tony'.

Of course, not all politicians are devious swine who sup on orphans' tears. Black nationalist Marcus Garvey, who suffered a fatal stroke in 1940 after reading a negative premature obituary of himself (wouldn't you?), is an enduring presence in reggae and hip-hop. Burning Spear dedicated a whole album to him; here's the righteous title track.

Zimbabwean Dorothy Masuka raises a joyous salute to a trifecta of post-independence African leaders (Ghana's Kwame Nkrumah, Kenya's Jomo Kenyatta and Congo's Patrice Lumumba), while indie trio Drugstore sing of Chilean president Salvador Allende's death during Pinochet's US-backed 1973 coup. When Pinochet was detained in London, protestors had the perfect soundtrack. That's Thom Yorke keening along, by the way.

And so to the Bush era, with punk-funk malcontents !!! protesting the future presidential hopeful's killjoy policies as mayor of New

York. There's a nice lyrical nod to Neil Young's Nixon-themed 'Campaigner', too. Spoilt for choice in the Bush-bashing stakes, I voted for the Legendary KO, who folded Kanye West's famous statement into his hit 'Gold Digger', added new lyrics, and produced this eloquent blast of post-Katrina rage. Finally, Jarvis's 'Running the World' names no names but its disgusted refrain – featuring a word you'll never hear on daytime radio – covers them all.

THE PLAYLIST

Exhuming McCarthy REM

The Old Man's Back Again (Dedicated to the Neo-Stalinist Regime) Scott Walker

You Haven't Done Nothin' Stevie Wonder

Whine and Grine / Stand Down Margaret The Beat

Marcus Garvey Burning Spear

Ghana Dorothy Masuka

El President Drugstore

Me and Giuliani Down By the School Yard (A True Story) !!!

George Bush Doesn't Care About Black People The Legendary KO

Running the World Jarvis Cocker

MULTILINGUAL
SONGS

(▶) Every year, media coverage of Eurovision reaffirms one of the fundamental assumptions underpinning British music's self-image, namely that pop in other tongues is intrinsically inferior, not to mention hilarious. Even as music becomes more polyglot (acts as mainstream as Air, CSS and Arcade Fire alternate languages with ease), the novelty factor lingers.

Perhaps it's because so many lyricists struggle to make sense in their native argot, let alone anyone else's. Full marks for effort to the Clash ('Spanish Bombs'), despite doing to the Spanish language what the Luftwaffe did to Guernica, and the Fall ('Bremen Nacht'), apparently using German gleaned exclusively from *Commando* comics: 'Ich raus schnell mach von Bremen Nacht.' *Achtung, Schweinhund! Hände hoch!*, etc. The most multilingual offering is Madonna's 'Sorry'. It seems she can now apologise for *Swept Away* in ten different languages.

Predictably, French produces the richest pickings, though whether that's a tribute to the unrivalled sophistication of the Gallic tongue or the legacy of compulsory French lessons I cannot say. Faced with changing the gender of Randy and the Rainbows' Denise, and understandably averse to Dennis, Blondie invented a French casanova called Denis, and sang a verse accordingly. Amorous exchange students took notes.

German industrial-metal band Rammstein slip into English to underscore their point about American cultural dominance on 'Amerika'. 'This is not a love song,' growls Till Lindemann. 'I don't sing my mother tongue.' Ukrainian-born New Yorker Eugene Hutz mixes Russian and English on 'Sally', a lusty manifesto for his multi-cultural gypsy-punk troupe. 'I ended up being walking United Nation,' he explains in an accent broader than the Dnieper.

Pixies' Frank Black frequently amplified his alien quality with manic bursts of Spanish but there's only room for one Anglo-Spanish entry, and that's 'Venceremos (We Will Win)', British jazzers Working Week's elegantly understated tribute to victims of the Chilean junta. Tracey Thorn, Robert Wyatt and Chile's Claudia Figueora swap verses. Continuing the South American theme, Brazil's Jorge Ben mixes Portugese and English on the breezy 'Take It Easy My Brother Charles'.

Now for some less commonly heard languages. Along with Super Furry Animals, Gorky's Zygotic Mynci flew the flag for the Welsh vernacular in the early 1990s. 'Patio Song' does so with unforced charm. Sigur Rós went one better, inventing a private lingo they called Hopelandic. The ecstatic 'Hoppípolla', which you'll recognise if you've seen any TV trailers in the past three years, combines it with their native Icelandic. On 'Satta Massagana', reggae trio the Abyssinians prove their devotion to the Rastafarian homeland of Ethiopia with a refrain in Amharic.

Bryan Ferry sang *auf Deutsch* on Roxy Music's 'Bitter-Sweet', but 'Song for Europe' is not only a better song; it has verses in French *and* Latin, which must be the least pop-friendly language of them all. *Enfin*, Blur's ravishing 'To the End', reworked as a fully bilingual duet with Parisian icon Françoise Hardy. *Et voilà, c'est tout.*

THE PLAYLIST

Denis Blondie

Amerika Rammstein

Sally Gogol Bordello

Venceremos (We Will Win) Working Week

Take It Easy My Brother Charles Jorge Ben

Patio Song Gorky's Zygotic Mynci

Hoppípolla Sigur Rós

Satta Massagana The Abyssinians

Song for Europe Roxy Music

To the End (La Comédie) Blur

SONGS ABOUT
ROADS AND STREETS

(▶)I'm no board game mogul, but it strikes me that the world needs a pop edition of Monopoly. You could start with the insalubrious blues and browns (Dead End Street, Electric Avenue), move through the mid-range locations (Penny Lane, Baker Street, Cyprus Avenue) and end up, like Kirsty MacColl, on Madison Avenue. En route you'd build Heartbreak Hotels and, if you were unlucky, go straight to Jailhouse Rock.

Although I've linked roads and streets here, they're opposites rather than allies. Streets are a destination; roads are a journey. Streets root you; roads release you. Streets impress their history upon you; roads are blank slates. I think that's why the former have inspired many more songs. They have better stories to tell.

Written by country singer John D. Loudermilk and inspired by the no-hope backwater in Erskine Caldwell's Depression-era novel, 'Tobacco Road' reeks of the American south. So who better to provide the definitive rendition than a group from Weybridge, Surrey? Nashville Teens' snarling boogie is as authentic as their name was bogus.

'Desolation Row', painted in vivid and cryptic strokes by Bob Dylan, might have had a literary source, too: Steinbeck's *Cannery Row*. Or maybe not. It's also been interpreted as referring to Duluth, Minnesota, Eighth Avenue, New York or bohemia. Perhaps it means nothing much and just sounded good one day in 1965. Still sounds good now, all eleven breathless minutes of it. Maybe he was getting paid by the word. During his burst of late 1980s positivism, Prince's spiritual home was the kaleidoscopic 'Alphabet St'.

Some immortalise where they came from (Paul Weller's *Stanley Road*, Rod Stewart's 'Gasoline Alley'), others where they're going. Back when New York, rather than LA, was the engine room of American pop, the Drifters sang of Broadway's bright lights, as well as the hard times awaiting the less fortunate. Donovan's eye-opening jaunts from St Albans to London spawned 'Sunny Goodge Street's dreamy beatnik musings: 'Listening to sounds of Mingus, mellow fantastic.' In 1929, Louis Armstrong waxed lyrical about Basin Street in his hometown of New Orleans.

The carpet-chewing insanity taking place on Echo and the Bunnymen's 'Villiers Terrace' suggests lysergic dementia, but it's apparently an abstruse reference to Hitler. Either way, it's one of their finest songs, electric with nervous energy. Give Gene Pitney an emotional molehill and he'd turn it into Everest. '24 Sycamore' is a break-up writ apocalyptic: 'I've just lost a lifetime / I have just lost my mind.' Morrissey's choice of Maudlin Street would be self-parodic (it's from *Carry On Teaching*) were the song not so magnificent: a farewell to the site of lost love that is evocative, witty and moving.

Time to leave town. The two definitive road songs are Bobby Troup's 'Route 66' and Kraftwerk's 'Autobahn': one buzzing with hotheaded American optimism, the other unflappable, futuristic and unmistakably German. Primal Scream credit both on their immaculate krautrock homage. Do pass Go. Do collect £200.

THE PLAYLIST

Tobacco Road Nashville Teens
Desolation Row Bob Dylan
Alphabet St Prince
On Broadway The Drifters
Sunny Goodge Street Donovan
Basin Street Blues Louis Armstrong
Villiers Terrace Echo and the Bunnymen
24 Sycamore Gene Pitney
Late Night, Maudlin Street Morrissey
Autobahn 66 Primal Scream

SONGS ABOUT
THE SEA

(▶) One night in 1971, a depressed Brian Wilson sat on a beach, gazing out and feeling desperately insignificant. The next day, he started writing ''Til I Die'. 'I wanted the music to reflect the loneliness of floating on a raft in the middle of the Pacific,' he later wrote. 'I wanted each note to sound as if it was disappearing into the hugeness of the universe.'

Even if you're not in such a parlous state of mental health as Wilson was, the sea can have that effect. In most songwriters' imaginations, it is immense, overwhelming and dreadfully lonely. Even the bawdiest sea shanties celebrated on 2006's *Pirates of the Caribbean*-inspired *Rogue's Gallery* compilation arose from the knowledge that not all the people singing them would live to see dry land.

Perhaps no theme has inspired fewer songs by black artists. The magnificent title track of the O'Jays' indignant masterpiece *Ship Ahoy* suggests one reason why, by describing the boats that brought slaves from Africa to the Americas. Introduced by the creak of timbers and the crack of whips, it weeps with anger.

Squawking seagulls herald Procol Harum's 'A Salty Dog', from the nautical concept album of the same name. Slightly strained lyrics aside, it's a rather lovely example of progressive rock before it drowned in its own pomposity. Cerebral metallers Mastodon based their *Leviathan* album on *Moby Dick* – the mighty 'Seabeast' cites Ahab and Queequeg – but I bet they skipped the chapter about how to make candles from whale tallow. Everyone skips that one. In recent years, none have embraced the ocean as enthusiastically as British Sea Power. 'Carrion' is a drowner's manifesto phrased in wonderful gusty poetry: 'From Scapa Flow to Rotherhithe / I felt the lapping of an ebbing tide.'

Countless maritime songs cover the gulf separating two lovers. Surely the jauntiest is Bobby Darin's light-footed Americanisation of Charles Trenet's 'La Mer'. In turn it inspired a hammy Robbie Williams cover and a misbegotten Kevin Spacey film but we shouldn't hold that against it. Folk singer Cyril Tawney served thirteen years in the Royal Navy, so he knew whereof he sang in 'The Grey Funnel Line': 'The finest ship that sails the sea / Is still a prison for the likes of me.' All About Eve cleave to folk's tradition of shivery longing on 'Martha's Harbour'.

Many songs take place at sea, but very few actually *in* it. Robert Wyatt's 'Sea Song' is truly aquatic, an extraordinarily odd and affecting love song to a woman whose 'madness fits in neatly with my own'. It sways like a boat before plunging into the eerie deep. Perhaps island races are particularly well attuned to the sea's rhythms. On 'The Anchor Song', Björk sits on the Icelandic shore and decides for once *not* to sail away.

We end where we began, with the Beach Boys, and a classic from the choppy waters of their 1970s career. Written largely by Brian Wilson's sympathetic ally Van Dyke Parks, it fashions confusion and despair into an improbably cheering cry of perseverance: 'Often frightened, unenlightened / Sail on, sail on sailor.'

THE PLAYLIST

Ship Ahoy The O'Jays
A Salty Dog Procol Harum
Seabeast Mastodon
Carrion British Sea Power
Beyond the Sea Bobby Darin
The Grey Funnel Line Cyril Tawney
Martha's Harbour All About Eve
Sea Song Robert Wyatt
The Anchor Song Björk
Sail On Sailor The Beach Boys

SONGS ABOUT
SILENCE

(▶) In early 2001, when guitar music seemed distinctly rudderless, at-a-loss music journalists cooked up a half-baked scene called the New Acoustic Movement, taking as its slogan the tongue-in-cheek title of a lovely, understated album by Norwegian duo Kings of Convenience: *Quiet is the New Loud*. It didn't catch on. Just as the new black is always black, the new loud will for ever be loud.

Like the Velvet Underground's 'Candy', pop tends to hate the quiet places. Its fundamental imperatives are to make some noise, to turn it up, to say it loud. Quiet too often leads to bland. But a few musicians rewardingly ponder the sound of silence, with its power to heal or to stifle. I toyed with including John Cage's famous '4'33"', but why waste a slot? Just sit there noiselessly for four minutes and thirty-three seconds after the playlist is over. *Voilà* – your own John Cage bonus track, absolutely free.

Some songs demand silence while making a racket, like Deep Purple's rattlingly good, career-launching assault on Joe South's 'Hush'. On tour together in 1978, Go-Go Jane Wiedlin and the Specials' Terry Hall sparked up a romance which inspired them to co-write the gossip-scorning 'Our Lips Are Sealed': 'There's a weapon / We must use / In our defence / Silence.' Hall subsequently recorded it with Fun Boy Three but the Go-Go's' version is new wave perfection. Not a single note is wasted.

When it comes to the virtues of saying less, there are only two contenders: the Beach Boys' 'Don't Talk (Put Your Head on My Shoulder)', and Depeche Mode's 'Enjoy the Silence'. Songwriter Martin Gore conceived it as a ballad until bandmate Alan Wilder and producer Flood, besotted with house music, opted to rework it as a soaring dance record. Its status as Depeche's best-loved song is down to that improbable alloy of introspection and euphoria.

Minnesota's Low, a band who used to perform so quietly that they risked being submerged by audience noise, play with contrast here, serenely pondering the upside of hearing loss ('We won't have to speak and we won't have to lie') before threatening the eardrums with a mighty squall of noise.

Silence can also disturb. The Knife's techno noir is stealthily terrifying, with a central image plucked straight from a bad dream. 'Your Silent Face' is quintessential New Order: exquisitely mournful electronic pop brought thumping to earth by a deadpan punchline: 'You've caught me at a bad time / So why don't you piss off.'

Plagued by noisy neighbours, soul singer Garnet Mimms begs for serenity on 'A Quiet Place', so let's treat him to the Cocteau Twins' rippling, beatific 'Lazy Calm' and the undulating currents of Miles Davis's jazz fusion benchmark 'In a Silent Way'. Ah, that's better. But Mimms might regret what he wished for when he hears 'No Surprises', a portrait of suburban ennui which seems to embrace a more final peace – a lullaby for the suicidal – because life with no alarms and no surprises is no life at all.

THE PLAYLIST

Hush Deep Purple

Our Lips Are Sealed The Go-Go's

Enjoy the Silence Depeche Mode

When I Go Deaf Low

Silent Shout The Knife

Your Silent Face New Order

A Quiet Place Garnet Mimms

Lazy Calm Cocteau Twins

In a Silent Way/It's About That Time Miles Davis

No Surprises Radiohead

RALLYING CRIES

▶ Anyone who's witnessed a huge concert and caught a hint of Nuremberg knows there is something faintly terrifying about the power wielded by a rock star. People have a primal need to feel part of something bigger than themselves, and if the man leading the chant is wearing jeans and a guitar strap rather than a uniform and armband, well, that's got to be an improvement.

What that chant actually consists of scarcely matters. In the blaze of the moment, a yelp of thrilling nonsense is no less potent than a revolutionary battle cry. One should always beware hubris. Liam Gallagher's preposterous command on 'D'You Know What I Mean' – 'All my people right here, right now' – was Britpop's 'Ozymandias' moment.

Talk of favourite lyrics tends to prioritise elaborate wordsmiths, but much though I savour a well-turned couplet, I suspect pop's lifeblood is the blunt, irresistible slogan: c'mon everybody; fight the power; get up, stand up; hey ho, let's go. So let's have MC5's fire-starting 'Kick Out the Jams' (has any song ever been blessed with a more electrifying introduction?) and Slade's ill-spelt glam-rock rampage 'Cum On Feel the Noize'.

M/A/R/R/S were indie dilettantes rather than electronic pioneers, but by raiding recent rap and house hits for the most urgent imperatives – 'Put the needle on the record!', 'Rock the house!', 'Pump up the volume! Dance! Dance!' – they were the ones who triggered Britain's dance music deluge. Public Enemy also made their point with canny sampling, reversing and radicalising the hook from the Beastie Boys' frat-rap anthem 'Fight for Your Right' alongside James Brown's stern command from 'Get Up, Get Into It, Get Involved'.

The Animals rewrote Barry Mann and Cynthia Weil's America-set 'We've Gotta Get Out of this Place' to allude to the claustrophobia of England's industrial north, only to see it acquire a completely different meaning among GIs in Vietnam. The Damned's 'Smash It Up' was punk stripped of Lydon and Strummer's political agenda and boiled down to the sheer, animal-brain joy of demolition. 'Glastonbury hippies' and 'frothy lager' are among their targets. Not usually famed for their milkman-friendly hooks, Stereolab produced an art-pop classic in 'French Disko's galloping cry of highbrow defiance: '*La résistance!*'

Here's one invitation which shouldn't be taken at face value, unless I've got this terribly wrong, and Leonard Cohen really did want his fans to march on Manhattan and Berlin. His unsettlingly droll excursion into the fevered imaginings of a terrorist mastermind casts a far more chilling spell now than it did in 1988. 'You know the way to stop me,' he rumbles, 'but you don't have the discipline.'

In case you're still sedentary, these last two should get you on your feet. Sly Stone's glorious 'Stand!' is an all-purpose resolve-stiffener, as personal or political as the listener wants it to be, while Arcade Fire's clarion call for perseverance against the odds, brought to a climax by Win Butler yowling 'You'd better look out below!', could raise the dead.

THE PLAYLIST

Kick Out the Jams MC5
Cum On Feel the Noize Slade
Pump Up the Volume (USA 12" mix) M/A/R/R/S
Party for Your Right to Fight Public Enemy
We've Gotta Get Out of this Place The Animals
Smash It Up (Parts 1 and 2) The Damned
French Disko Stereolab
First We Take Manhattan Leonard Cohen
Stand! Sly and the Family Stone
Wake Up Arcade Fire

RURAL
SONGS

(▶) I'll admit right now that I'm not the country type. The fields I tend to end up in contain PA systems, falafel vans and men in colourful trousers touting magic mushrooms. When people eulogise the space and quiet of the English countryside, I just find myself thinking: *Yes. And?*

I reckon I have pop on my side. It is, in Charlie Gillett's memorable phrase, the sound of the city, born amid concrete and smoke, informed by the clatter of industry, always thrusting towards the future. In music, the country represents the past, taking the listener back before rock 'n' roll's big bang, to the dirt roads of blues and the green fields of folk.

There is so much folk to choose from. Reluctantly snubbing Vashti Bunyan, Pentangle and a field of John Barleycorns, I've picked the Watersons' Trad Arr *a cappella*, 'Country Life'. You won't find a more bucolic vision this side of the industrial revolution. By way of contrast, Bow Wow Wow head for the hills to wriggling Latin rhythms.

The Band's 1968 debut album introduced a rootsy, back-to-the-land spirit to US rock, which spawned a drearily persistent obsession with authenticity and the infuriating good-life solipsism of the LA

Canyon scene, but they weren't to know it would turn out that way. From their second album, King Harvest's evocative, Steinbeck-inspired tale of 1930s farm labourers must have come as a gust of fresh air.

Two rural childhoods remembered, in two different countries. Burning Spear celebrates the daily routine of water-collecting and fire-building in hilly inland Jamaica, thus demonstrating that the only thing mellower than reggae is pastoral reggae. On the Go-Betweens' best-loved song, Grant McLennan recalls himself at different ages, wending home through the sugar cane fields of northern Queensland. Over in Mali, Ali Farka Touré mourns the parched demise of the West African savannah.

The flight from a small town is one of rock's classic narratives, but the narrator of New Model Army's 'Green and Grey' is someone left behind, penning resentful letters to an escapee. Even though the rural northern life he describes is a deadening cycle of punch-ups and downpours, he makes staying there a point of perverse pride: 'Do you think you're so brave just to go running to that which beckons to us all?' A stirring, conflicted song from a band that is too often simplistic.

Talking Heads in '(Nothing But) Flowers' imagined a mechanised America undone by nature, its malls standing empty and overgrown. Grandaddy, situated where Silicon Valley meets the wilds of California, find similar resonance in the image of discarded consumer goods: 'Meadows resemble showroom floors / Owls fly out of oven doors.'

Boards of Canada are the masters of agrarian techno. 'In a Beautiful Place Out in the Country' has an uncanny, rusted melancholy – a soundtrack for androids dreaming of electric sheep. Finally, twittering birdsong heralds Pink Floyd's Arcadian idyll, flooded with the hazy, hypnotising warmth of a perfect English summer.

THE PLAYLIST

Country Life The Watersons
Go Wild in the Country Bow Wow Wow
King Harvest (Has Surely Come) The Band
Man in the Hills Burning Spear
Cattle and Cane The Go-Betweens
Savane Ali Farka Touré
Green and Grey New Model Army
Broken Household Appliance National Forest Grandaddy
In a Beautiful Place Out in the Country Boards of Canada
Grantchester Meadows Pink Floyd

HOMOSEXUALITY

(▶) Asked once why he waited until 1994 to come out, Neil Tennant replied that he was wary of being typecast as 'gay pop star Neil Tennant'. One can understand his concern. I don't buy the Boy George line that a gay musician's responsibility to be honest overrules the artistic right to ambiguity. Pop thrives on mystery and speculation. When that goes the meaning of a song can become pinned like a butterfly, where before it was fluttering and elusive.

For that reason, I've tried to concentrate on the song rather than the singer. Dusty Springfield's sexual preferences don't automatically make 'The Look of Love' a gay song, any more than Suede's 'The Drowners' stands or falls on who Brett Anderson slept with. Anyway, sexuality, as the openly gay yet fortunately untypecast Michael Stipe has said, 'is a really slippery thing'.

There's not a scintilla of ambiguity in Elton Motello's thrillingly filthy 'Jet Boy, Jet Girl', which hijacks 'Ça Plane Pour Moi' (Motello's band played on the 1978 Plastic Bertrand hit) with lyrics like 'I'm gonna make you penetrate / I'm gonna make you be my girl.' Franz Ferdinand, our token straight act, play the old Bowie/Suede homo-eroticism game on the fierce, sweaty 'Michael'.

Pete Shelley's post-Buzzcocks synth-pop single 'Homosapien' was banned by the BBC for its 'explicit reference to gay sex'. Considering how touching and elegant the lyrics are, one can only imagine what the corporation made of Elton Motello. We've got to have a Tennant lyric in here somewhere. The brilliant 'Can You Forgive Her?' portrays a closeted gay man irate because his girlfriend knows he's in denial.

From the much smaller canon of lesbian songs, Lucille Bogan's 1930s blues strut 'B.D. Woman's Blues' is simply extraordinary: the B.D. stands for Bull Dyke. Weezer's Rivers Cuomo wished the object of his affection wasn't gay on 'Pink Triangle' ('If everyone's a little queer / Can't she be a little straight?'), and Sophie B. Hawkins describes the reverse scenario on the uncommonly heated AOR of 'Damn I Wish I Was Your Lover', with its memorable invitation to 'come inside my jungle book'.

Perhaps the only songwriter on Earth who makes Rufus Wainwright seem coy is the Hidden Cameras' Joel Gibb. This is a ballad as tender as it is explicit, making even the image of a lover 'peeing on my shoulders and knees' sound impossibly romantic. On 'Breathing Fear', Kitchens of Distinction condemn homophobia with subtlety and grace. At a time when Morrissey was (as he remains) coy about his sexuality, singer Patrick Fitzgerald was the only openly gay man in indie-rock, which was a mixed blessing. 'The gay issue became a huge red herring,' he later reflected. 'A pink herring, in fact! The "gay thing" insinuated the music was different to what it was.'

For our grand finale, Marc Almond changes the nature of Charles Aznavour's 'What Makes a Man a Man' from empathetic character-study to quasi-autobiography, and Carl Bean crafts the most candid and life-affirming gay anthem in the disco songbook, which is saying something.

THE PLAYLIST

Jet Boy, Jet Girl Elton Motello
Michael Franz Ferdinand
Homosapien Pete Shelley
Can You Forgive Her? Pet Shop Boys
B.D. Woman's Blues Lucille Bogan
Damn I Wish I Was Your Lover Sophie B. Hawkins
The Man That I Am With My Man The Hidden Cameras
Breathing Fear Kitchens of Distinction
What Makes a Man a Man Marc Almond
I Was Born This Way Carl Bean

SONGS ABOUT
THE ENVIRONMENT

(▶) I assembled this playlist the week of Live Earth, an event doomed to generate little besides hot air. For one thing, staging an enormous, carbon-spewing, eight-city series of rock gigs to raise awareness of green issues seemed rather like holding a hog roast to promote vegetarianism. For another, if someone had managed to remain ignorant of environmental crises thus far, then it was doubtful that Razorlight were going to enlighten them.

Notwithstanding Duran Duran's chutzpah in attempting to pass 'Planet Earth' off as an eco-anthem (by that logic, was 'Rio' a prophetic reference to the 1992 climate summit?), songs about the environment were an endangered species at the concert. Thirty-seven years after Marvin Gaye's 'Mercy Mercy Me (The Ecology)', a record so pioneering that Motown boss Berry Gordy didn't even know what *ecology* meant, explicitly green songs are out of fashion. Perhaps songwriters were scared off by Michael Jackson's loopy 'Earth Song'. 'What about elephants?' What indeed?

Once Marvin, Neil Young and others had put the environment on pop's agenda at the dawn of the 1970s, even the toothsome Osmonds were inspired to release a gloriously berserk anti-car rant. *Cra-zee hor-ses! Wreee! Wreee!* Makes me smile every time. Rather more sophisticated is the Pixies' marvellous 'Monkey Gone to Heaven', which explains global warming in the chillingly simple language of a children's fable: 'Now there's a hole in the sky / And the ground's not cold / And if the ground's not cold / Everything is gonna burn.'

On 'Supernature', Franco-disco *grand fromage* Jean Marc Cerrone prophesied pesticide-spawned mutants exacting gruesome revenge upon humanity, a scenario which for some reason has thus far eluded Al Gore's attention. Coldcut built 'Timber' from video clips of deforestation (you can see it on YouTube), splicing rainforest chants with the deadly percussion of axes and chainsaws. A protest song without lyrics – quite a feat.

REM were the 1980s' most consistently eloquent pop eco-warriors. Witness 'Cuyahoga', 'Turn You Inside Out', or this soaring commentary on acid rain. Michael Stipe once deemed 'Fall On Me' his favourite REM song, back when he was a shrewd judge of such things. From the Byrds' distinctly spotty post-1970 catalogue comes the smouldering 'Hungry Planet', which is far better than a song narrated by an aggrieved Earth has any right to be.

More apocalyptic still is Orbital's 'Impact (The Earth Is Burning)' – climate change as it might be envisioned by the writers of *Dr Who*. Amid wild, overheating acid house, a panicky voice cries out: 'It's a cry! A cry for survival! For them and for us!' Meanwhile, Julian Cope spies disaster on the motorway on this Cassandra-like track from his car-crushing concept album *Autogeddon*.

Even Joni Mitchell is tired of 'Big Yellow Taxi', the overplayed eco-ditty she wrote during a disheartening trip to Waikiki (perhaps she heard Counting Crows' ghastly cover and cursed what she had unleashed upon the world), but its airy charm keeps it fresh. Finally, the Handsome Family imagine Mitchell's forlorn scenario reversed by resurgent nature: it overgrows parking lots and puts up paradise.

THE PLAYLIST

Crazy Horses The Osmonds

Monkey Gone to Heaven Pixies

Supernature Cerrone

Timber Coldcut

Fall On Me REM

Hungry Planet The Byrds

Impact (The Earth Is Burning) (USA version) Orbital

Autogeddon Blues Julian Cope

Big Yellow Taxi Joni Mitchell

Peace in the Valley Once Again The Handsome Family

SWEARY
SONGS

(▶) It is eighteen years since Tipper Gore's Parents Music Resource Center started slapping CDs with stickers reading Parental Advisory Explicit Content (which, naturally, became a badge of honour for any self-respecting rapper), but a swear word on a record still has the power to shock if it's used in the right way.

Ten songs are nowhere near sufficient to trace the full history of swearing in pop, which would start with X-rated blues outtakes, stop off at the 1965 debut album by garage-rock mischief-makers the Fugs and come up to date with Amy Winehouse's ingenious application of 'fuckery'.

In assessing good cussing, let's not underestimate the petulant and the juvenile. Just as Eamon's 'Fuck It (I Don't Want You Back)' encapsulates the incoherent rage of a spurned teenager, Rage Against the Machine's 'Fuck you, I won't do what you tell me' is the truest variety of rebel yell. Spare a thought for the hapless DJ Bruno Brookes, who once played the uncensored version on tea-time Radio 1.

Where do you start with hip-hop? While admiring Ra the Rugged Man's gleefully offensive 'Cunt Renaissance' – the smack of Anglo-Saxon and Latinate words in unlikely collision – I've picked Pharoahe

Monch's mighty 'Simon Says', on no account to be confused with the children's game. Back when swearing on a pop record was simply inconceivable, some musicians amused themselves with absurdly raunchy private takes, never to be heard in public. Posterity is indebted to whoever rescued Jackie Wilson and Lavern Baker's hilarously filthy private version of 1965 hit 'Think Twice' from the studio floor. Older still is 'Good Ship Venus', a collection of bawdy pirates' limericks revived on 2006's *Rogue's Gallery* compilation. Guess what Venus rhymes with.

The Sex Pistols recorded their own version under the name 'Friggin' in the Riggin', but the howlingly bleak 'Bodies' was the track which shocked and thrilled young purchasers of *Never Mind the Bollocks*, while announcing John Lydon as one of pop's champion swearers. More historically significant profanity courtesy of John Lennon: the stark, bitter delivery of 'fucking peasants' – from a former Beatle, no less – still punches the gut.

Ra the Rugged Man's favourite expletive sounds doubly fierce coming from a woman; pity the adulterous scoundrel who inspired Marianne Faithfull's toxic ire. Although the boldness of Canadian electro-rapper Peaches is overrated by people who have never heard Lil' Kim, 'Fuck the Pain Away' is her best song, poised between self-empowerment and self-destruction.

Finally, two monuments to repetition. John Cooper Clarke bowdlerised his poem 'Evidently Chickentown' when he recorded it, substituting a 'bloody' for every 'fucking', but the point is the same: language as relentlessly ugly and impoverished as the environment it describes. We end where we began, on a note of potty-mouthed protest, as the Super Furry Animals loop one Steely Dan lyric into a galloping battle cry. The 2004 live version repeats the title phrase around 100 times, which, if you ask me, is a bit fucking much.

THE PLAYLIST

Killing in the Name Of Rage Against the Machine
Simon Says Pharoahe Monch
Think Twice (Version X) Jackie Wilson and Lavern Baker
Good Ship Venus Loudon Wainwright III
Bodies Sex Pistols
Working Class Hero John Lennon
Why'd Ya Do It? Marianne Faithfull
Fuck the Pain Away Peaches
Evidently Chickentown John Cooper Clarke
The Man Don't Give a Fuck Super Furry Animals

FLIGHT

(▶) I think it's important to remember the pleasures of flying – the first glimpse of a new city at night, the first breath of unfamiliar air, the complimentary pretzels – but it's getting harder. If the snowballing security checks don't smash the last atoms of glamour out of air travel, then the eco-guilt will.

This is where music's power to summon magic from the mundane comes in. Who wants to hear a song about removing your shoes at the X-ray machine, or choosing between chicken and beef? (Sole exception: Saint Etienne's 'Mr Donut', a homesick ballad named after a fast-food franchise popular in Japanese airports.) Music can revive the dream of flying – the idea that mankind's ability to soar above the clouds is, despite all the petty irritations, a wondrous thing.

Back in 1957, commercial air travel was still radiant with romance, particularly, I imagine, if you were Frank Sinatra. Buoyed by Billy May's breezy arrangement, 'Come Fly with Me' invites boomtime America to join the good life: 'If you can use some exotic booze / There's a bar in far Bombay.' Flying would never again sound as fun. Trust the Specials to capture the jetlag jitters of the tour-weary band on 'International Jet Set': 'A vapour trail from A to B, away from normal sanity.'

The Byrds wrote 'Eight Miles High' about their first trip to London (lyricist Gene Clark suffered dreadful aviophobia), but Roger McGuinn's lysergic, Coltrane-inspired guitar solo led some censorious radio stations to deem it a drug song. For a change, here's Hüsker Dü's version, a groundbreaking union of hardcore punk and psychedelia which inspired the title of the Flaming Lips retrospective *Finally, the Punk Rockers Are Taking Acid*. Named after a forgettable Yul Brynner movie about US rescue pilots in Japan, Kaleidoscope's 'Flight from Ashiya' paints turbulence in the phantasmagorical colours of a bad trip. Motörhead's 'Bomber' sounds like a warplane glowering overhead.

We now leave the cabin (placing our tray tables in the upright position) for two abstract flights. Jazz-folk innovators Pentangle take a gravity-defying excursion on 'Light Flight', while the slippery space-funk of Steve Miller Band's 'Fly Like an Eagle' promises escape from poverty, allegedly in reference to native American reservations.

With musicians away from home so much, no wonder the aeroplane becomes a symbol of separation and reunion. Unlike poor Gordon Lightfoot, stranded on the tarmac in 'Early Mornin' Rain', Alison Goldfrapp travels 'miles and miles of sun' to be with her beloved on this decade's most sumptuous synth-pop record. Joni Mitchell turns to the ghost of vanished aviator Amelia Earhart to confide the regrets of a life ruled by wanderlust: 'I've spent my whole life in clouds at icy altitude.' Exquisitely sad.

Gruff Rhys's 'Skylon!' opens with a cabin announcement, before embarking on a rambling, hilarious narrative about a TV personality, a terrorist and a bomb disposal expert, complete with York Study Notes-style recap at the twelve-minute mark. Which leaves just one crucial question hanging in the air: chicken or beef?

THE PLAYLIST

Come Fly with Me Frank Sinatra
International Jet Set The Specials
Eight Miles High Hüsker Dü
Flight from Ashiya Kaleidoscope
Bomber Motörhead
Light Flight Pentangle
Fly Like an Eagle Steve Miller Band
Fly Me Away Goldfrapp
Amelia Joni Mitchell
Skylon! Gruff Rhys

SONGS ABOUT
POVERTY

(▶) Listening to dozens of records about having nowt, I found myself imagining a musical version of Monty Python's Four Yorkshiremen sketch. 'We used to live in t'ghetto,' says Gil Scott-Heron. 'You were lucky you had a ghetto,' retorts Woody Guthrie. 'We had to live in a dustbowl.' 'Dustbowl?' sniffs Big Bill Broonzy. 'We used to dream of living in a dustbowl.'

The Four Yorkshiremen were right, though. Poverty *is* relative. The impoverished Malawians whom Lucius Banda chronicles in 'Mzimu wa Soldier' would gaze longingly at the hovel inhabited by the protagonists of the Smiths' 'Jeane', while the dissolute narrator of the Kinks' 'Sunny Afternoon' hasn't got a leg to stand on.

In the 1920s, Blind Alfred Reed's repertoire included an anti-flapper tirade called 'Why Do You Bob Your Hair, Girls?', which makes this number less a protest song than an inspired grumble, signed, Disgruntled of West Virginia. Reed sings it with brisk indignation, as if jabbing his finger into the listener's chest.

The parlous state of America's inner cities informed soul's greatest era. Stevie Wonder and Marvin Gaye's inner-city blues are well-known, but the overlooked 'Hard Times' is just as moving, written by Curtis Mayfield and sung by a clinically obese Chicago singer who suffered a fatal heart attack before the track was even released. In 1969, you'd have struggled to find a performer further from the ghetto than Elvis, but the memory of his own hardscrabble upbringing gave 'In the Ghetto' enough authentic emotion to save it from being the 'Another Day in Paradise' of its time.

Over in London, Ray Davies never joined the 1960s party. For the denizens of 'Dead End Street', scraping together 'a Sunday joint of bread and honey', the only thing swinging is the laundry in the wind. Where would the Jam have been without it? Desmond Dekker is a put-upon family man in a song that only younger listeners can hear without picturing a certain low-fat spread, and Creedence's John Fogerty is a penniless itinerant musician in 'Lodi': 'If I only had a dollar for every song I've sung . . . I'd catch the next train back to where I live.'

Two different punk responses to penury. Gang of Four find a short-term solution – 'To hell with poverty! We'll get drunk on cheap wine' – on an influential disco-punk rampage which still sounds fresh today. The Dead Kennedys' blackly ironic 'Kill the Poor' ('unsightly slums gone up in flashing light') is a three-minute update of Jonathan Swift's 'A Modest Proposal', intentional or otherwise.

Richard and Linda Thompson haunt the sunless tenements, bringing dire tidings: 'Most of the people are poor in the heart / It's the worst kind of poor you can be.' Then it's back to the days of Blind Alfred Reed, with Bessie Smith's caustic reflections on the Wall Street

Crash and the fickleness of friendship. Down and out? We used to dream of being down and out.

THE PLAYLIST

How Can a Poor Man Stand Such Times and Live?
   Blind Alfred Reed

Hard Times Baby Huey

In the Ghetto Elvis Presley

Dead End Street The Kinks

Israelites Desmond Dekker and the Aces

Lodi Creedence Clearwater Revival

To Hell with Poverty! Gang of Four

Kill the Poor The Dead Kennedys

The Sun Never Shines on the Poor Richard and
   Linda Thompson

Nobody Knows You When You're Down and Out
   Bessie Smith

AFRICA

(▶) Some pieces of music are so thoroughly wrong-headed that, in retrospect, you wonder whether they really existed, or were just some kind of bizarre aural hallucination. One such piece is the jingle for a 1980s soft drink. 'Um Bongo, Um Bongo, they drink it in the Congo,' chanted the cartoon animals, because nothing says fruity refreshment quite like a century or so of slavery, tyranny, genocide and war. Amazingly, it's still available on the brand's website, although claims of Um Bongo consumption in the Congo region remain unconfirmed to this day.

I was reminded of it while YouTubing the video to Toto's notorious soft-rock calamity 'Africa'. Sure as Kilimanjaro rises like Olympus above the Serengeti, it stinks. It would seem that it took Stephen Biko's murder to persuade white musicians that Africa was not, in fact, a giant safari park. There are good records which use the continent as an exotic locale without making your toes curl, but to exclude an African song to make room for, say, Madness's 'Night Boat to Cairo' didn't seem right.

The first song dates back to 1897. Written by Xhosa schoolteacher Enoch Sontonga, 'Nkosi Sikelel'i Afrika (God Bless Africa)' is the national anthem for no fewer than three countries: Zambia, Tanzania and (partially) South Africa. It knocks 'God Save the Queen' into a cocked hat, but then what doesn't?

Lord Kitchener, a Trinidadian with a calypso for every occasion, celebrated Ghana's 1957 declaration of independence under president Kwame Nkrumah. A shame he (Nkrumah, not Kitch) was deposed nine years later by a US-backed coup. Working in Los Angeles in 1969, Fela Kuti surveyed his troubled homeland on 'Viva Nigeria', an unusually concise example of his nascent afrobeat sound. He later regretted this sop to the government – the message of unity implicitly rebukes Biafran separatists – but its spry optimism still charms.

Few records are as redolent of the British left in 1985 as Latin Quarter's 'Radio Africa', the musical equivalent of an earnest student meeting in the Nelson Mandela bar. The brisker version they later recorded with Zimbabwe's Bhundu Boys has aged much better. Consequently, the playlist's token white face belongs to former Van der Graaf Generator frontman Peter Hammill, who recites a fractured history of African despotism over nerve-jangling, mechanised post-punk which grumbles like a knackered engine.

Jamaica in the 1970s saw a rash of so-called repatriation songs, seeking spiritual salvation in a return to an idealised motherland. Billy Paul's exquisite 'East' is the Philly soul equivalent: half lament, half prayer. The Congos' Lee Perry-produced 'Congoman' goes one better by *sounding* like central Africa: dense and humid. A decade earlier,

Art Blakey and his crack squad of jazz drummers tried to evoke the continent on a fine album called *The African Beat*.

We should end with something from African music's current purple patch. Canadian-based rapper K'naan acidly contrasts everyday strife in his native Somalia with the gangsta boasts of American MCs, while Sahara bluesmen Tinariwen hymn the nomadic Tuareg lifestyle with what Andy Kershaw memorably described as 'roll 'n' roll music'. Somebody send Toto a copy.

THE PLAYLIST

Nkosi Sikelel'i Afrika Soweto Gospel Choir

Birth of Ghana Lord Kitchener

Viva Nigeria Fela Kuti

Radio Africa Bhundu Boys (with Latin Quarter)

A Motor-Bike in Afrika Peter Hammill

East Billy Paul

Congoman The Congos

Obirin African (Woman of Africa) Art Blakey and the
    Afro-Drum Ensemble

What's Hardcore? K'naan

Amassakoul 'n' Ténéré Tinariwen

SMILING AND LAUGHING

(▶) In his song 'What's Wrong with This Picture?', Lloyd Cole neatly skewers the miserabilist mindset: 'Smile, she said, and if you want / I'll look the other way / Till you regain your melancholy disposition / Or until you get over yourself.'

That self-serious pose is common to both adolescents and songwriters, and you can hardly blame them. While there is a rich and complex vocabulary for sadness, joy is more elusive. Hats off to anyone who can write a song about smiles or laughter that isn't either maddeningly perky or secretly barbed. In the first category resides Shanice's 'I Love Your Smile', listening to which is like gargling sugar-water at gunpoint. In the second, we find the Supernaturals' 'Smile', superfically the acme of Britpop jollity, but actually as bleak as Bergman: 'I feel like a Dalek inside.'

The most vexing thing a depressed person can hear is 'Cheer up', but Nat King Cole's voice is so deeply reassuring it could be used as a crowd-calming measure. Here, he's wise enough to appreciate all the reasons not to smile and optimistic enough to recommend you do anyway. A half-century later, that same attitude ignited Gnarls Barkley's 'Smiley Faces': 'You know how hard this life can be / But you keep on smilin' for me.'

'Tears of a Clown's aggressively cheerful circus-style intro (written by Stevie Wonder) sets up Smokey Robinson's final, faultless refinement of a conceit he'd already used on 'Tracks of My Tears' and Carolyn Crawford's 'My Smile is Just a Frown (Turned Upside Down)'. If there are any clowns who come home from a hard day spent hurling custard pies and climbing out of under-sized cars and don't break down sobbing at the emptiness of it all, then we never hear about them.

Steve Harley's biggest hit is also deceptively upbeat. He can say that it's a poison pen letter to ex-bandmates until he's blue in the face, but people will still dance to it at weddings, not least because it has the best false ending in pop. Likewise The The's brilliant 'Uncertain Smile': loveless late-night moping masked by a sparkling melody.

From the Bee Gees' terribly earnest early days, Robin Gibb's quavering parable of a misunderstood martyr is humourless and florid but, not for the first time, his gift for a tune redeems everything. The jangling black comedy of Josef K's 'Sorry for Laughing' makes an apt contrast.

The Undisputed Truth were Motown hitmaker Norman Whitfield's pet band: a testing ground for his new songs and a court of appeal for his undervalued old ones. 'Smiling Faces Sometimes', reclaimed from the Temptations, was their sole chart success, a miniature masterpiece of crawling paranoia.

On the dissipated funk of *There's a Riot Goin' On*, even the hits have queasy undercurrents. '(You Caught Me) Smilin' has a seductive decadence, Sly singing with the semi-apologetic charm of a junkie caught in the act: 'You ain't used to seein' me turned on.' Playing us out, folk wit John Prine mischievously endorses a narcotically assisted grin. What would Nat King Cole say?

THE PLAYLIST

Smile Nat King Cole

Smiley Faces Gnarls Barkley

Tears of a Clown Smokey Robinson and the Miracles

Make Me Smile (Come Up and See Me) Steve Harley and Cockney Rebel

Uncertain Smile The The

I Started a Joke The Bee Gees

Sorry for Laughing Josef K

Smiling Faces Sometimes The Undisputed Truth

(You Caught Me) Smilin' Sly and the Family Stone

Illegal Smile John Prine

SONGS ABOUT
RADIO

(▶) The day I realised that I was no longer strictly young was the day I switched my alarm clock from Radio 1 to Radio 4 (it was Chris Moyles's fault). Instead of waking up to pop music and gibberish, I now open my eyes to the sound of John Humphrys, a man who seemingly regards popular culture as if he has just peeled it off his shoe and is holding it at arm's length until a suitable means of disposal can be found.

I'll know I'm old when I no longer listen to pop radio at all. Now that consumer choice is the media's prevailing obsession, there is something indescribably magical about hearing a song, old or new, that you *haven't* chosen, while knowing that thousands of unknown fellow listeners are having the same experience, far away yet intimately connected.

Most of the great radio songs were recorded when the medium was unchallenged by video channels or the internet. Whether it was seen as a companion for the lonely (the Carpenters' 'Yesterday Once More'), a generational unifier (Reunion's 'Life Is a Rock (But the Radio Rolled Me)'), or the mouthpiece of the corporate beast (Elvis Costello's 'Radio Radio'), it was inescapable. Even now that its power is diminished, at least the Buggles were wrong: the radio star endures.

Before they discovered robots, Kraftwerk communed with more mundane machinery. 'Radioland' makes the act of turning a dial to produce music (hear the squiggling, frequency-surfing sound effects) seem as miraculous as it should. More AM celebration from Jonathan Richman, speeding through the Massachusetts night, egged on by the Modern Lovers' jubilant cry of 'Radio on!' The Replacements lend tattered romance to the early 1980s indie rock scene with 'Left of the Dial': that's where the college radio stations could be found.

Meat Beat Manifesto imagine the signature tune of an under-ground station on 'Radio Babylon', all fathomless bass and dub-meets-rave drum clatter. Wilco's *Yankee Hotel Foxtrot* album was obliquely inspired by numbers stations, those mysterious broadcasters transmitting coded messages to Cold War spooks. The concept informs 'Radio Cure', eerie and sad: 'My mind is filled with radio cures / Electronic surgical words.'

Of all the songs damning mainstream radio playlists ('hang the blessed DJ', indeed), my favourite is the sole moment of pop genius from two-tone B-listers the Selecter. Rush, usually given to outré sci-fi concept albums, also struck pop gold with 'The Spirit of Radio', juggling the comforts of radio ('Undemanding contact / In your happy solitude') with the corruption of commerce (they'd know about that), over gleaming, FM-ready rock. Indeep pay disco homage to the power of the late-night DJ. There ain't a problem that he can't fix, 'cause he can do it in the mix.

Lastly, two songs for lovers. In her spine-shivering 'On the Radio', Regina Spektor enjoys an unlikely epiphany hearing Guns 'n' Roses' 'November Rain' over the airwaves while poor Bryan Ferry is ambushed by a song pouncing out of the car radio to remind him of lost love. Fade to static.

THE PLAYLIST

Radioland Kraftwerk
Roadrunner The Modern Lovers
Left of the Dial The Replacements
Radio Babylon Meat Beat Manifesto
Radio Cure Wilco
On My Radio The Selecter
The Spirit of Radio Rush
Last Night a DJ Saved My Life Indeep
On My Radio Regina Spektor
Oh Yeah Roxy Music

NORTHERN ENGLAND

(▶) In any contest to find pop's most northern lyric, my money would be on the line in 'Fake Tales of San Francisco' where Alex Turner reminds a Strokes-a-like wannabe, 'You're not from New York City, you're from Rotherham.' It's not just the tart candour and bathetic delivery: it's the attitude that you should embrace where you're from, despite – no, because of – its dearth of glamour.

It's impossible to imagine the situation in reverse. Even avowed anglophiles like Interpol have never bluffed intimate knowledge of Salford or Macclesfield. New York or London are partly cities of myth, dreamed to life by fascinated outsiders. The north is seen with clearer vision, almost exclusively by people born there.

No songwriter looks to the north for glitz. The horny-handed retiree in traditional folk song 'The Dalesman's Litany' bids good riddance to the forges, mines and dark satanic mills: 'From Hull, Halifax and Hell, good Lord deliver us.' 'It's Grim Up North', by a pseudonymous KLF, wrongfoots the listener. A deadpan catalogue of northern towns, recited over rainy-motorway techno, suddenly blossoms into a rendition of Blake's 'Jerusalem', as if arriving at some socialist rave utopia.

While songs such as the Smiths' 'London' and the Pet Shop Boys' 'Being Boring' describe leaving the north, Elbow's 'Station Approach' brilliantly recreates a return journey, with familiar streets scrolling past through train windows: 'I need to be in the town where they know what I'm like and don't mind.' The Animals wittily relocate 'Gonna Send You Back to Georgia', Timmy Shaw's waspish dismissal of a smalltown girl spoilt by the big city, to the Newcastle suburb of Walker. The Fall, plagued by sinister visions, hear 'the induced call, mysterious – hit the north'.

'I Predict a Riot' deserves a mention, not least for introducing the word *Leodensian* to pop's lexicon, but freakbeat minnows Wimple Winch (you'll have to forgive the name) got there first, foreseeing sozzled aggro in 1960s Stockport. If they'd had Booze Britain in 1967, this would have been the theme tune. There's more strife in the Icicle Works' dystopian epic about beleaguered 1980s Liverpool: 'We used to pull the ships in / Now we're going down.'

What about life outside the cities? The Charlatans classic described by Tim Burgess as 'a song about all your dreams coming true' immortalises the Cheshire village of Sproston Green. Escape velocity is attained via the late Rob Collins's heroic Hammond organ solo. OMD are Kraftwerk with a view of Ellesmere Port rather than Düsseldorf, pondering a feckless lover beneath the comforting permanence of Stanlow oil refinery. The plant itself seems to provide the clanking beat.

What with the Arctic Monkeys, Pulp and Richard Hawley, one is spoilt for both droll and poetic evocations of Sheffield, but here's a neglected heartbreaker from Monkey Swallows the Universe, watching the rain fall 'so much that the seven hills became seven seas' and softly dreaming of sailing their house 'from Fulwood to High Green'. It came out in 2006; a year later, Sheffield flooded for real. Were they trying to tell us something?

THE PLAYLIST

The Dalesman's Litany Tim Hart and Maddy Prior
It's Grim Up North The JAMMs
Station Approach Elbow
Gonna Send You Back to Walker The Animals
Hit the North The Fall
Rumble on Mersey Square South Wimple Winch
Up Here in the North of England The Icicle Works
Sproston Green The Charlatans
Stanlow Orchestral Manoeuvres in the Dark
Sheffield Shanty Monkey Swallows the Universe

SONGS ABOUT
FOOD

(▶) In a parallel universe, one of the most famous songs in the world is called 'Scrambled Eggs'. That was the working title Paul McCartney used while working out a melody on a hotel piano in January 1964. Once he'd come up with some proper lyrics, the song was rechristened 'Yesterday'. Good news for pop: bad news for the popularisation of breakfast options.

As McCartney demonstrated, food is what you sing about when you're waiting for something better to come along. Whereas coffee, wine and cigarettes have all been used as poignant metaphors, food seems too prosaic, too *messy*, to carry serious emotional weight. It's the stuff of novelty records, in-jokes and instrumentals, some good (the Beatles' 'Savoy Truffle' is an enjoyable bit of fluff), some dreadful (the Undertones' clunky 'Mars Bars' is displeasure you can't measure).

Early jazz musicians were a hungry lot but none covered as many bases as Cab Calloway, who assigned a rhyming comestible to each of his house guests. Plato gets fobbed off with a tomato; you'd think one of the fathers of philosophy deserved better than that. The Flaming Lips have a broad streak of psychedelic whimsy. The stirringly nonsensical 'She Don't Use Jelly' celebrates a woman who spreads her guests' toast with vaseline, so Plato could have done worse. Much worse in fact; he could have had Funkadelic's unappetising 'Fish, Chips and Sweat'.

Going all the way back to Bessie Smith's thinly coded 'I Need a Little Sugar in My Bowl', food has been a hard-working double entendre. Kelis continued the tradition with 'Milkshake' and not for the first time. She also sang the lip-lickingly flirtatious hook on rapper Foxy Brown's Neptunes-produced 'Candy' and it's every bit as good. As well as sex, victuals can stand for cash. Wu-Tang Clan member Raekwon knits together two slang terms, ice (cocaine) and cream (money), on this brooding drug-dealer narrative.

When you're titling instrumentals, anything goes. The Just Brothers recorded 'Sliced Tomatoes' (famously employed as the spine of Fatboy Slim's 'The Rockafeller Skank') and saxophonist Preston Love made a whole album of barbecue-themed grooves. The daddy of them all is Booker T. and the MGs' 1962 hit 'Green Onions'. Brian Wilson's drug-blitzed eccentricity reached full flower on the goofy yet lovely 'Vegetables', first written for his aborted *Smile* album. You could pick Wilson's 2004 version but the original boasts the sound of Paul McCartney (him again) chomping celery. Robert Wyatt goes one stranger on the jaunty, jazzy 'Soup Song' by personifying a piece of bacon aggrieved at being relegated to a broth flavouring. Not a metaphor: literally a piece of bacon.

Regional cuisine lends a song extra flavour. Hank Williams plans a big date in New Orleans on 'Jambalaya (on the Bayou)' while dub kingpin Lee 'Scratch' Perry tucks into a Jamaican menu on 'Roast Fish and Cornbread'. Finally, Goldfrapp are at their most heart-rendingly opulent on 'Black Cherry's five minutes of erotic rapture. No, she doesn't mean the yoghurt flavour.

THE PLAYLIST

Everybody Eats When They Come to My House   Cab Calloway

She Don't Use Jelly   The Flaming Lips

Candy   Foxy Brown feat. Kelis

Ice Cream   Raekwon

Green Onions   Booker T. and the MGs

Vegetables   The Beach Boys

Soup Song   Robert Wyatt

Jambalaya (on the Bayou)   Hank Williams

Roast Fish and Cornbread   Lee 'Scratch' Perry

Black Cherry   Goldfrapp

SONGS ABOUT
CELESTIAL BODIES

(▶) Wayne Coyne of the Flaming Lips once reminisced to an interviewer about being eight in 1969: watching the moon landings, listening to his older brothers' psychedelic rock, and being absolutely, positively convinced that one day he and everyone he knew would be living in space. Well, you would, wouldn't you?

I don't imagine NASA timed Apollo 11 to coincide with the release of the Grateful Dead's 'Dark Star', but the whole endeavour remains the modern era's crowning example of science feeding art. Far from being dimmed by scientific discovery, space's mystery is enhanced by it – the more we learn, the more we marvel. For a songwriter, especially one in an altered state, it is hard to resist the ready-made metaphor of the light from a dead star, or that phenomenon peculiar to the Oasis nebula, the champagne supernova.

Syd Barrett was Pink Floyd's first starry-eyed voyager, but when he got lost in space, Roger Waters charted his own course for the heart of the sun, taking inspiration from Chinese poetry and John Coltrane in true 1968 style. Muse compress prog-rock's grandiose conceits into ultra-dense pop songs. If Prince had been a Rush fan, 'Supermassive Black Hole's implosion of intergalactic lust might have been the result.

Space travel has never sounded as light and whimsical as it does on

Bart Howard's standard 'Fly Me to the Moon', though apparently spring on Jupiter and Mars isn't all it's cracked up to be. Julie London's pizzicato-powered version out-zings Sinatra's. Philly soul keyboardist Dexter Wansel cashed in on the mid-1970s vogue for all things spacey with the sci-fi disco of 'Life on Mars', while across the Atlantic Hawkwind aimed for a far-off spiral galaxy with the kind of lustrous, mellotron-powered space rock that kept the lava lamp industry in business.

Back on Earth, Brian Eno and John Cale watch the constellations form a 'million insect storm' in the darkening sky. 'Spinning Away's theme is art outpaced by nature, and the disorientating wonder of a universe in constant motion. Another awestruck stargazer is the eccentrically gifted Patrick Wolf, illuminating his observation of Orion and Ursa Major with twinkling keyboards and lancing rays of drum 'n' bass. 'Look up! The stars!'

In space nobody can hear you sob. *Planet* comes from the Greek word for *wandering star*, a poetic image rendered hideously lonely by Portishead, whose Beth Gibbons is a loveless outcast set adrift, in a direct quote from the Book of Jude, amid 'the blackness of darkness forever'. Middle-of-the-night music if ever there was.

Sydney band the Church struck gold in 1988 with a deft trick of scale, panning back from faltering romantic manoeuvres in a rock venue named after the Milky Way, Amsterdam's Melkweg, to imply the looming vastness of the real thing. Beth Orton no longer shows any inclination to make ten-minute-long depressive dub-folk, more's the pity. 'Galaxy of Emptiness' is so exquisitely evocative that it deserves to be heard on a clear night beneath the stars.

THE PLAYLIST

Set the Controls for the Heart of the Sun Pink Floyd

Supermassive Black Hole Muse

Fly Me to the Moon Julie London

Life on Mars Dexter Wansel

Spiral Galaxy 28948 Hawkwind

Spinning Away Brian Eno and John Cale

The Stars Patrick Wolf

Wandering Star Portishead

Under the Milky Way The Church

Galaxy of Emptiness Beth Orton

MISSING SOMEONE

(▶) A few years ago, my wife went to Australia for a month and I made her a tape which included Etienne Daho's 'Me Manquer', an unabashedly sentimental Air-remixed ballad with the simplest chorus: 'I miss you.' Over the phone, she jokingly accused me of emotional sadism because she couldn't hear it without welling up. In my defence, nor could I.

Missing someone, even if you know they're coming back, is exquisitely painful. Do we listen to pertinent songs to soothe the pain or sharpen it? Is that distinction even possible? When we hear 'Wichita Lineman' or 'Nothing Compares 2 U', we feel better because someone else knows how much it hurts, and worse because they express it all too well.

Before the inevitable heartbreak, a pre-emptive strike: the 13th Floor Elevators' hair-raising adolescent howl of narcissism, insecurity and spite. Terry Callier's rippling folk-funk delivery of the same message is calmer and more deadly; producer Charles Stepney's horns jab the ungrateful lover like an accusing forefinger.

Roughly ninety per cent of pop is either about wanting someone, having them, or losing them and wanting them back. Hal David's lyric to 'I Just Don't Know What to Do with Myself' earns its playlist slot by nailing the way that when you miss someone, you're missing a piece of yourself. Dusty's definitive version ascends from shellshock to epic desperation in three dizzying minutes. Was there ever a club anthem bleaker than 'Missing'? Tracey Thorn haunts the darkened streets looking in vain for a vanished ex; thanks to remixer Todd Terry she haunted 1990s dancefloors too.

For couples who are still together but not *together*, it's a waiting game. 'Clouds Across the Moon', a Brit-soul curio written by journeyman arranger/composer Richard Anthony Hewson and sung by his wife, is a gimmicky conceit (woman speaks via satellite to astronaut husband) with a surprisingly poignant bite. Thank Mrs H.'s cut-glass tones, betraying just the faintest wobble of the upper lip. For Death Cab for Cutie, the Atlantic might as well be deep space. Frontman Ben Gibbard pines while gusting guitars prepare to make landfall.

Dylan wants to be casual and magnanimous on 'If You See Her, Say Hello', but the resentment leaks – no, *floods* – through. By the final lines, he's talked away all the dignity he pretended he had. Likewise, the unreliable narrator of 'I Get Along Without You Very Well' (an amateur poem turned into a jazz standard by Hoagy Carmichael) dismantles the title's claim verse by verse. Chet Baker's version stands alone: androgynous, ethereal, like a ghost sighing in the autumn leaves.

What thunderbolt of inspiration struck Gary Barlow the day he wrote 'Back for Good', and why did it never return? Simply the greatest boy-band ballad since the Jackson 5 broke up, but 'got your lipstick marks still on your coffee cup'? Do some washing up, man; pull yourself together. As a final caustic antidote to all of the above, Dan Hicks wisecracks 'How Can I Miss You When You Won't Go Away?' Well, quite.

THE PLAYLIST

You're Gonna Miss Me 13th Floor Elevators

You're Goin' Miss Your Candyman Terry Callier

I Just Don't Know What to Do with Myself Dusty Springfield

Missing (Todd Terry remix) Everything But the Girl

Clouds Across the Moon The R.A.H. Band

Transatlanticism Death Cab for Cutie

If You See Her, Say Hello Bob Dylan

I Get Along Without You Very Well Chet Baker

Back for Good Take That

How Can I Miss You When You Won't Go Away? Dan Hicks and His Hot Licks

MUSICAL INSTRUMENTS

(▶) As a former bass guitarist, albeit one with no discernible musical talent, I was delighted to discover 'Mr Bass Man', Johnny Cymbal's 1963 tribute to 'the hidden king of rock 'n' roll', and crestfallen to realise that it referred to the bass *singers* in 1960s vocal groups. You're short of options when you're the band member traditionally described as 'dependable'.

Bassists aren't alone though. Less rock-friendly musicians have to seek out Serge Gainsbourg's 'Black Trombone' or the Birthday Party's 'Mr Clarinet', while the poor kazoo player must forage around in verse two of Creedence Clearwater Revival's 'Down on the Corner'. Meanwhile, the guitar is lavished with love. The Cowboy Junkies' was blue, David Sylvian's was red, George Harrison's cried like a baby and Steve Earle's had a whole damn town named after it. No wonder guitarists tend to develop ego problems.

I miss the tradition of band leaders introducing all the instruments one by one. In his musical kitchen, King Curtis gathers his ingredients: half a teacup of bass, a pound of fatback drums, a little pinch of organ. I think Arcade Fire should adopt this tactic. Lighten the mood a bit.

Country singer Jerry Reed scored his first hit (swiftly covered by Elvis) with a spirited anthem for all America's guitar-slinging hopefuls, while the Lemon Pipers' nugget of psychedelic bubblegum spoke up for struggling street musicians. Unkind listeners might suggest the busker's fortunes would be improved if he learned a proper instrument rather than just banging a tambourine.

Mike Nesmith's 'Different Drum' was a product of its time: an earnestly high-flown excuse for the inability to resist shagging anything in range (see also 'Free Bird' and 'Love the One You're With'). The Lemonheads lend it just the right amount of roguish charm. Ill-starred former Byrd Gene Clark earned Bob Dylan's respect with his gorgeous, cryptic meditation on the Spanish guitar.

Brandished by Jimmy Page in 'The Song Remains the Same', the hurdy gurdy became a symbol of intolerable hippie pretension, as indeed did most of Donovan's lyrics, but the song still has an acid-dazed brilliance, largely thanks to the session work of three future Led Zeppelin members. Maybe that's where Page got the idea. In Nick Cave's savagely funny retelling of Orpheus inventing the lyre, the instrument becomes a stringed killing machine. Understandably annoyed at being slain, Eurydice welcomes her husband to the underworld with the words, 'If you play that fucking thing down here I'll stick it up your orifice!'

Hip-hop turned a mechanism for playing music into a tool for making it, a seismic innovation celebrated by Beck in 'Where It's At's joyous chorus: 'Two turntables and a microphone.' Instrumentals like Mike Oldfield's 'Tubular Bells' or the Hollywood Persuaders'

'Drums-A-Go-Go' can be good advertisements for certain devices, though Aphex Twin's thrilling 'Didgeridoo' emulates the instrument's warbling drone by entirely electronic means. Penguin Café Orchestra's Simon Jeffes came across a discarded harmonium in a Tokyo street and was inspired to create his best-loved tune. He's lucky he didn't find a kazoo.

THE PLAYLIST

Memphis Soul Stew King Curtis and the Kingpins
Guitar Man Jerry Reed
Green Tambourine The Lemon Pipers
Different Drum The Lemonheads
For a Spanish Guitar Gene Clark
Hurdy Gurdy Man Donovan
The Lyre of Orpheus Nick Cave and the Bad Seeds
Where It's At Beck
Didgeridoo Aphex Twin
Music for a Found Harmonium Penguin Café Orchestra

NIGHT AND DARKNESS

▶ Some records are like vampires: they shrivel on exposure to daylight. Play an album like Frank Sinatra's *In the Wee Small Hours*, or Burial's self-titled dubstep masterpiece, beneath bright blue skies and hear its power drain away, but put it on in the dead of night and it will engulf you.

We are not concerned here with the bright, companionable nights that Morrissey longs for in 'There Is a Light that Never Goes Out' ('Where there's music and there's people / And they're young and alive') but with the cases where the lights *do* go out, when your only company is the music itself.

Mercury Rev's *All Is Dream* album unfolds with the eerie, unreal exaggeration of the midnight river journey taken by the children in Charles Laughton's *Night of the Hunter*. 'The Dark Is Rising' sets the mood: sporadically an orchestra ignites, like flares shooting up into the sky, before fluttering down like embers, leaving frontman Jonathan Donahue as frail and lonely as before.

In Frankie Valli's fraught Motown hit, the night is baleful henchman to a sinister love rival. Klaxons' 2007 cover version revealed excellent taste but a failure to realise when perfection had already been achieved. The young Françoise Hardy faces a moment of emotional reckoning on the darkened boulevards of Paris in 'La Nuit Est sur la Ville'.

For some, the night is an accomplice, the darkness enfolding them like a pair of black, protecting wings. In the Five Satins' doo-wop classic, you can imagine the teenage lovers sheltering from the prying eyes of censorious 1950s parents. In the soul standard 'The Dark End of the Street', two adulterers can only express their love in the shadows. Songwriters Dan Penn and Chips Moman dashed it off during a DJ convention in Memphis, where the fabulously named Goldstar boss Quinton Claunch promptly snapped it up for James Carr. Folk-rockers the Youngbloods embrace darkness in a spirit of denial, imploring it to 'take away the pain of knowing', as if life were just a long, cruel bout of insomnia.

A night-time playlist without goths would be like Ant without Dec. Bauhaus, often dismissed as cartoon bat-botherers, rip through 'Dark Entries' like they've been up for three nights and are still too wired to sleep. Don't be fooled by the daft title Sufjan Stevens gave to his apparition of Illinois's resentful undead, who 'tremble with the nervous thought of having been, at last, forgot'. It's creepy and affecting.

British pianist Stan Tracey based his 1965 jazz suite on phrases from Dylan Thomas's *Under Milk Wood*, 'Starless and Bible Black' being the standout. It has the conspiratorial quality of so much after-hours jazz, the instruments murmuring to each other as though exchanging coded messages. Finally, the lushest, most nocturnal track from DJ Shadow's 1990s classic *Endtroducing*. Rarely have samples sounded so much like the restless ghosts of old records searching for new homes. Listen with the lights out.

THE PLAYLIST

The Dark Is Rising Mercury Rev
The Night Frankie Valli and the Four Seasons
La Nuit Est sur la Ville Françoise Hardy
In the Still of the Night The Five Satins
The Dark End of the Street James Carr
Darkness, Darkness The Youngbloods
Dark Entries Bauhaus
**They Are Night Zombies!! They Are Neighbors!! They Have
  Come Back from the Dead!! Ahhhh!** Sufjan Stevens
Starless and Bible Black The Stan Tracey Quartet
Midnight in a Perfect World DJ Shadow

LAW ENFORCEMENT

(▶) Spare a thought for the self-esteem of the music-loving policeman. In song after song, the cop is a rapper-harassing, punk-whomping, innocent-arresting, donut-eating creep. As Black Flag yowled in 'Police Story', 'They hate us, we hate us / We can't win.' Wait a minute, Fugazi's 'Great Cop' sounds promising. But no: it's just someone informing his girlfriend that her bullying suspicion makes her the perfect candidate for a career in law enforcement.

What's interesting about plod-bashing pop is how much it reveals about the times. Before punk, bands balked at openly slamming the police, but abuse of Britain's sus laws provoked responses from the Clash, the Ruts and Linton Kwesi Johnson, while the corruption and brutality of the LAPD brought us NWA's 'Fuck tha Police' and Body Count's 'Cop Killer'. In one of hip-hop's stranger ironies, Body Count's Ice-T now plays an officer on *Law and Order: SVU*.

Trust Bruce Springsteen, at least, to see the working man behind the badge. The tense, Suicide-inspired 'State Trooper' puts a sinister twist on his well-worn open-road motif by placing a desperate fugitive at the wheel, fearing for the fate of anyone unlucky enough to pull him over. 'Maybe you got a kid,' he mutters. 'Maybe you got a pretty wife.'

Unlike the furiously indignant NWA, Cypress Hill strike a note of mocking contempt on their infectious gangsta nursery rhyme: 'Well this pig's standin' eatin' donuts / While some motherfucker's out robbin' your home.' Mudhoney uncork a gallon of bile on their cover of 'Hate the Police' by Texan punks the Dicks.

The violence that engulfed Jamaica in the late 1970s inspired an epidemic of songs about police harassment. Notwithstanding the Clash's clenched-fist interpretation, Junior Murvin's 'Police and Thieves' is less a cry of anger than a sigh of disappointment, sung in an airy falsetto that seems to float above the whole seething mess. Alex Turner also stands apart from the fray as the wry observer of closing-time aggro on 'Riot Van'.

The Pet Shop Boys set the secret police to synth-pop on 'In the Night' but Abba got there first. On the title track from their swansong album, a hunted Eastern Bloc dissident cowers from a knock on the door; paranoia never sounded so jaunty. McCarthy, described by Nicky Wire as 'the great lost band of the 1980s', thrived on the disjuncture between Malcolm Eden's acidic Marxist critique and Tim Gane's toothsome melodies. This satirical manifesto for state violence is cloaked in sunny jingle-jangle. Humour of a broader variety from Bo Diddley, who was as much a comic storyteller as a rock 'n' roll singer.

Neil Young taps into his inner Dylan on 'Crime in the City (Sixty to Zero, Pt 1)', a cryptic meander through benighted streets where idealism withers, innocents suffer and the policemen become indistinguishable from the crooks. Finally, Mike Post's classic *Hill Street Blues* theme serves reminder that at least there's one place where the police are almost always right: TV. Right, Ice-T?

THE PLAYLIST

State Trooper Bruce Springsteen

Pigs Cypress Hill

Hate the Police Mudhoney

Police and Thieves Junior Murvin

Riot Van Arctic Monkeys

The Visitors (Crackin' Up) Abba

The Home Secretary Briefs the Forces of Law and Order
   McCarthy

Cops and Robbers Bo Diddley

Crime in the City (Sixty to Zero, Pt 1) Neil Young

Hill Street Blues Mike Post and Larry Carlton

PHYSICAL ILLNESS

▶ A recent study (carried out, if I remember rightly, by the Department of Obviousology at No Shit University) found that rock stars tend to die younger than ordinary folk. But the roll call of premature rock fatalities is so littered with suicides, overdoses and plane crashes that an illness that could afflict anyone – Tammi Terrell's brain tumour at twenty-four or Minnie Riperton's cancer at thirty-one – seems somehow more shocking.

Despite pop's ample supply of doctors (Dre, Feelgood, Octagon, Hook), illness is rarely addressed except in the context of bereavement, though some obscure afflictions do make an appearance. Cowboy Junkies' 'Mining for Gold' mentions scoliosis, Radiohead named an album after the bends, and Huey 'Piano' Smith publicised the little-known maladies rockin' pneumonia and boogie-woogie flu. At the time of writing, there is still no cure for disco fever.

Faced with such a gloomy topic, let's start light. Scratch-happy DJ Kid Koala cuts together a beat from coughs and sneezes on 'Flu Season', while Big Bill Broonzy takes the tradition of sickbed blues ('TB Blues', 'Dust Pneumonia Blues') to ludicrous extremes: '"Oh doctor, what you gon' do with that saw?" / "Oh, we take off legs with that, that's all."'

More gallows humour as Madness cheerfully prescribe rest to a harried salaryman on 'Cardiac Arrest', only to watch him crumple to the ground in the final verse. Brighton's Fujiya and Miyagi titled 'Collarbone's krautrock-indebted funk after vocalist David Best's childhood fractures. His variation on the old spiritual 'Dem Bones' can't help but recall the menacing white-coated chorus line in *The Singing Detective*.

As shown in Anton Corbijn's astutely titled biopic *Control*, Ian Curtis wrote 'She's Lost Control' after the fatal seizure of an epileptic job-centre client, using her fate as a focus for the powerless dread that his own epilepsy inspired: 'She expressed herself in many different ways / Until she lost control again.' Cole Porter phrased love as an infection in 'I've Got You Under My Skin', which Neneh Cherry reinterpreted half a century later as an eerie, breakbeat-backed metaphor for HIV/AIDS.

Misleadingly adopted as a soundtrack to the death of the Britpop party, 'The Drugs Don't Work' was really a response to Richard Ashcroft's father's cancer. Despite one lyrical hiccup (a cat in a bag doesn't exactly *wait* to drown, does it?), it's the most graceful and moving song he ever wrote. Van Morrison is another helpless hospital visitor on the insidious blues of 'TB Sheets'.

Roger Waters's 1970s obsession with the deadening effects of fame and wealth was tiresome in the extreme, but 'Comfortably Numb', inspired by his experience with anti-hepatitis tranquillisers, is so elegant in its immensity, and so exquisitely sinister in its medical vocabulary, that one resists the temptation to play the world's smallest violin. Finally, Regina Spektor beautifully describes a US cancer patient who decides to spend her money on living well, rather than longer: 'I couldn't afford chemo like I couldn't afford a limo / And on any given day I'd rather ride a limousine.'

THE PLAYLIST

Flu Season Kid Koala

Terrible Operation Blues Big Bill Broonzy

Cardiac Arrest Madness

Collarbone Fujiya and Miyagi

She's Lost Control Joy Division

I've Got You Under My Skin Neneh Cherry

The Drugs Don't Work The Verve

TB Sheets Van Morrison

Comfortably Numb Pink Floyd

Chemo Limo Regina Spektor

BIBLICAL
SONGS

(▶) In their anti-censorship satire 'Should the Bible Be Banned', indie agitators McCarthy imagine a fratricide blaming his actions on the story of Cain and Abel, prompting angry protestors to ask, 'Should the Bible be banned to keep the peace?' Good question. Any child with even the most cursory exposure to the Bible (I only studied the greatest hits in RE) will have encountered thousands of deaths by fire, flood, war, plague, crushing, beheading and crucifixion before they get the slightest whiff of a violent movie.

It's the fear and trembling, rather than the love and forgiveness, that exercises such a hold on the imaginations of songwriters such as Bob Dylan, Nick Cave and Tom Waits. Language this ancient and blood-stained is hard to resist. Whether, as listener or songwriter, you actually believe it is moot, on which point I'll echo the diplomatic dissent of *Porgy and Bess*'s Sportin' Life: 'It Ain't Necessarily So'.

Tired of being told by their masters that God wanted them to shut up and keep working, America's slaves were understandably drawn to the Bible's fiercer passages, where tyrants were humbled and walls came tumbling down. Like many spirituals, 'Joshua Fit de Battle of Jericho' is a coded protest song. If God were black, he'd sound like

Paul Robeson (if white, then Johnny Cash). Cecil B. DeMille rather than Exodus inspired Metallica's murderously heavy account of the plague of the firstborn.

It's a measure of the distance U2 travelled from *October*'s spartan piety to *Achtung Baby*'s dark mischief that Bono could retell the betrayal at Gethsemane as a churning, homoerotic break-up song narrated by Judas. The Boo Radleys' boldest and best song takes nothing from the gospels but its title, but that nod to the world's most famous comeback conspires with the soaring trumpet hook to turn the defeatist lyrics on their head. If Joni Mitchell had been a heroin-addicted former prostitute, she'd have been Judee Sill, whose wondrous 'Jesus Was a Cross Maker' frames romantic disappointment in biblical irony.

Back to the Old Testament for Pixies' 'Gouge Away'. P.J. Harvey, Regina Spektor and the Grateful Dead have also reworked the Samson story (rock has a thing for long hair) but none with such disconcerting humour and bloody zeal. The Congos' righteous masterpiece *Heart of the Congos* has a biblical reference at every turn; 'La La Bam-Bam' mellifluously recounts misdeeds from Genesis, Daniel and Matthew.

And so, inevitably, to Revelation. Blind Willie Johnson, whose deathly rasp is one of music's most bone-chilling sounds, greets the prospect with disturbing relish on 'John the Revelator'. Greek prog-rockers Aphrodite's Child, whose ranks included a pre-*Blade Runner* Vangelis and a pre-*Abigail's Party* Demis Roussos, devoted a whole album, *666*, to the end of days, and 'The Four Horsemen' is the wildly psychedelic highlight. To end the playlist on a less apocalyptic note, here's 'Jesus Christ', a college-rock Christmas classic from Big Star's falling-apart-at-the-seams period, which teeters uncertainly between sincerity and sarcasm. You'll be relieved to hear that nobody dies.

THE PLAYLIST

Joshua Fit de Battle of Jericho Paul Robeson

Creeping Death Metallica

Until the End of the World U2

Lazarus The Boo Radleys

Jesus Was a Cross Maker Judee Sill

Gouge Away Pixies

La La Bam-Bam The Congos

John the Revelator Blind Willie Johnson

The Four Horsemen Aphrodite's Child

Jesus Christ Big Star

OTHER SONGS

▶ Songs are time capsules. Crack them open years later and you find memories of a heady teenage summer, or a brief romance, or a friend you no longer see. So you get a special frisson when characters in songs have the same experience: the Knife, remembering corny adolescent dreams of erotic surrender to Berlin's *Top Gun* theme ('Take My Breath Away'), or Gillian Welch, recalling a love affair soundtracked by Steve Miller's 'Quicksilver Girl' ('My First Lover').

Songwriters mention specific songs for other reasons: to critique, to analyse, to homage, to spoof. In 'High Water (for Charley Patton)', Bob Dylan weaves himself into the tapestry of America's musical heritage. In 'You Were Right', Built to Spill reflect on the harsh wisdom that can sometimes be found in pop lyrics. But always we are reminded that music-makers are, first and foremost, music fans.

Adopting an existing song title is easy, but 'God Save the Queen' doesn't so much borrow its name as abduct it, pressing it, screaming, into the service of an inverted national anthem. The title is the crowning impertinence, though Malcolm McLaren claims that John Lydon 'wanted it to be called 'No Future'. I said, "That sounds like an ad for a bank." '

The French have a wonderful phrase for songs of retaliation: *chansons de revanche*. When Neil Young damned Alabama as a racist backwater under governor George Wallace, Lynyrd Skynyrd hit back with the fiery southern rock apologia 'Sweet Home Alabama', and Warren Zevon replied to *that* song with the scathing 'Play It All Night Long'. DJ Vadim's 'Your Revolution' critiques hip-hop culture from within, as poet Sarah Jones adapts Gil Scott-Heron ('your revolution will not happen between these thighs') and deflates famously priapic rap lyrics.

When David Bowie released *Low*, Nick Lowe wittily called his next EP 'Bowi'. On this subsequent hit, he sings about one song from *Low* ('Breaking Glass') while approximating another ('Sound and Vision'). More Top 10 intertextuality from Orange Juice, whose 'Rip It Up' namechecks the Buzzcocks' punk benchmark 'Boredom', paraphrases the lyrics *and* mimics the guitar solo.

Some songs become emblems of pop success: mountains to be climbed. Deep Purple pledge their love to rock 'n' roll by quoting Little Richard hits, while Sparks' hero is an embittered non-entity who dreams of being big enough to sing 'My Way', whether it be by flying as high as Sinatra or as low as Sid Vicious. The hyperarticulate Jeffrey Lewis bemoans the gulf between himself and the man who wrote 'Chelsea Hotel #2': 'If I was Leonard Cohen or some other songwriting master / I'd know to first get the oral sex and then write the song after.'

'The Ballad of Dorothy Parker' is the only time Prince sounds truly disorientated by sex, the music slip-sliding woozily beneath him. No wonder Joni Mitchell's on the radio singing 'Help me, I think I'm falling.' At home for Christmas, Okkervil River's Will Sheff hears Otis Redding crooning 'I've got dreams to remember', and is sent spinning back through his own memories – because, as we know, that's what a song can do.

THE PLAYLIST

God Save the Queen Sex Pistols
Sweet Home Alabama Lynyrd Skynyrd
Your Revolution DJ Vadim and Sarah Jones
I Love the Sound of Breaking Glass Nick Lowe
Rip It Up Orange Juice
Speed King Deep Purple
When Do I Get to Sing 'My Way' Sparks
The Chelsea Hotel Oral Sex Song Jeffrey Lewis
The Ballad of Dorothy Parker Prince
Listening to Otis Redding at Christmas Okkervil River